DAISY NGOZICHUKWUKA OBI

✝

PSALM

91

NINETY-ONE TIMES

Books Academy LLC
112 SW H K Dodgen Loop,
Temple, Texas 76504
Hotline: (254) 800-1189

Ordering Information:
Quantity sales. Special discounts are available on quantity purchases by corporations, associations, and others. For details, contact the publisher at the address above.

Printed in the United States of America.

ISBN-13:   Softcover   978-1-966567-07-3
              eBook   978-1-966567-08-0

Library of Congress Control Number: 2024926586

DEDICATION

ALL GLORY and honor, power, majesty, dominion with thanksgiving be unto my Lord and Savior JESUS Christ in the power of the Holy Spirit without whose guidance this unique book project will not have been possible. Praise God.

I dedicate this book to my beloved parents who are in heaven, Chief Senator ZC & Mrs Victoria Uduego (nee Princess Orizu) Obi, whose spiritual nurture in the Word of God, and benevolent nature grounded me to a maturing mental, and physical robust healthy life in the Lord.

"I will say always of the Lord, You are my refuge and my fortress, my God in whom I trust from everlasting to everlasting in Jesus Mighty Name."Amen! and Amen!

TABLE OF CONTENTS

FOREWORD

To God be the glory!

God has been on our side! If God had not been on our side, this book would not have been possible. The Spirit of God, the power that made the resurrection of our Lord

and Savior has made this original work possible. The Holy Spirit has been tugging in my heart to publish 91 versions of PSALM 91 for over two decades. I'm thankful that God did not give up on me.

Finally with the help of my research assistant in the person of my godson Believe, the Holy Spirit helped us to put it together. Believe Opara, I thank you for being such a blessing.

I thank Reverend Shorimade in locating a worthy printer at the last minute and thank the printers for being God's instrument in making this miracle project possible.

Heavenly Father, Your faithfulness and mercy endures forever. We are saying THANK YOU JESUS! Glory to God from everlasting to everlasting! I dedicate this book to you Almighty Father, to whom all glory belongs!

Amen!

Daisy Ngozichukwuka Obi

Daisy Obi, Pastor, Adonai Bible Center Massachusetts

To God be the glory! The mercy of God overwhelms me.

Our God is overflowing with compassion and kindness. In Palms 145 the Lord brings us home to who He is, an aspect of who he is as we read verses 8-9: The LORD is gracious, and full of compassion; Slow to anger, and of great mercy. The LORD is good to all; And his tender mercies are over all his works.

Yes, the Lord is FULL of mercy and compassion. It appears the LORD's mercy to me is greater than to others. See why I think so. A few years ago, and when I say a few, I believe like two to the decade ago, the Lord put the hunger and desire in my heart to do a project on Psalm Ninety-one. And there are several reasons for that. My parents, especially my earthly father raised us his children on the Psalms and Proverbs. Of course I did not know why he loved the Psalms and proverbs. He gathered us his household including the less privileged children who were temporarily adopted in our home because their parents were too poor to afford to take care of them or those children were orphans so they needed a good Christian home to grow up where their basic human needs can be met including basic education and spiritual nurture. My parents were very strong on biblical value like we find in Mark 12:29-31:

And one of the scribe came, and having heard them reasoning together, and perceiving that he had answered them well, asked him, which is the first commandment of all? And Jesus answered him, The first of all the commandment is, Hear, O

Israel: The Lord our God is one Lord: and thou shalt love the Lord they God with all thy heart, and with all thy mind, and with all thy strength; this is the first commandment. And the second is like, namely this, Thou shall love thy neighbor as thyself. There is none other commandment greater than these.

My father raised us on the King James Bible. We gathered as a family early in the morning and last thing before we retired to sleep to read the Bible and to read Psalm to pray. As far as I remember, no matter the Bible studies we read, we also read the Psalms and Proverbs especially Psalm Ninety-One. I remember one day, my mother requested me to read the Psalm Ninety-One every day on my own and I will see a special miracle in my life. I believe it was a word of knowledge and I believed my mother and started reading Psalm Ninety-One everyday and to this day, I read Psalm Ninety-One and Psalm Twenty-Three, many times each day and I have witnessed a lot of miracles as a result. Praise the Lord.

I believe my salvation manifested and I fully surrendered my life to Christ as a result of listening to my mother counseled me to read Psalm Ninety-One daily. That was over five decades. Over the years, God has taken me deeper into the knowledge of Him due my obedience in honoring my mother's spirituality.

I seem to own it now. Every end of the year like December 31, I read Psalm Ninety-One; Ninety-One times, the whole day, It used to take me the whole day and it was such a blessing to my life and my church members and all those that God has blessed to follow my teaching and believe God for great miracles and breakthroughs.

I come from a family with great faith in the efficacy of the word of God. My parents believe uncompromisingly that what God spoke and promised that he is able to do if we dare stand on it.

Thanks be to God that Jesus obediently gave His life to rescue us from the shackles of sin and death that "whosever believes in Him shall not perish but have everlasting life..."Amen

Do you know every word of God from Genes to the Book of Revelation is very important but the Word of God in your mouth id the one God uses to give you a breakthrough. Putting the Bible under your pillow may be a good habit but I when you open the inside pages and speak forth in faith to receive what has given you in your heart for that moment od need is what you give you the breakthrough you need for great victory. The Word of God works from the moment you work it. If you say you are a believer but only talks and never fellowship with our heavenly Father then it is only empty noise. God cannot be mocked. I choose to believe God rather than those who said they prayed and nothing happened. God cannot lie. The Bible say that God hears us when we call upon Him. The Bible says to call upon the Lord in the day of trouble and He will answer us.

Psalm 50:14-15 - Offer unto God thanksgiving; and pay thy vows unto the most high: And call upon me in the day of trouble: I will deliver thee, and thou shalt glorify me.

There are many scriptures to edify you in this are but Id give you just a few more and you can run with it and put the enemy on the run. Here are just a few - 1 Chronicles 4:10, Psalm 118:5, Psalm 4:1, ! John 5:14-15, Hosea 4:6, Joshua 1:8-9, Jeremiah 1:12, Isaiah 1:19. Psalm 91:1

Psalm 91 to me compasses many insights of the whole Bible.

Every verse of Psalm 91 has practically every face of the 66 Books of the whole Old and New Testament and this is a revelation direct from God. There are other Psalms that have great insights from God for me such as Psalm 23, 103, 121, 145. 46, 8, but Psalm 91 has such an inner strength of God for me.

All scripture is, according to 11 Timothy 3:16-17 All Scripture is given by inspiration of God, and is profitable for doctrine, for reproof, for correction, for instruction in righteousness: that the man of God may be perfect thoroughly furnished unto all good works. Amen! However, you cannot use all scripture simultaneously to meet all your needs.

At the same time, I know many Christians who say they have problems 'memorizing' scriptures. I remember Bro Kenneth Hagin remind us, his students at Rhema that does not demand us to do what we cannot do. He will be unjust and God is not unjust. Remember in Joshua 1:8 God, commanded Moses to teach Joshua when he was handing over to him (Joshua), not to let the Word of God depart out of his (Joshua) mouth, but to "meditate" in it always, constantly, day and night, think about it, remember it, turn it in his heart, sleep it, sing it, reflect it, form part of his (Joshua) DNA, eat it, drink it, dream it, run with it, pass it on, obtain victory with it, bring it to God, remind God of His Word, Remind God of His Covenant because He is a Covenant keeping God. Amen and Amen

Psalm 91 is that bulldozer of the Word of God which the Holy Spirit spoke through St Paul in Ephesians 6:10-20

Finally, my brethren, be strong in the Lord, and in the power of his might. Put on the whole armor of God, that ye may be able to stand against the wiles of the devil. For we wrestle not against the rulers of the darkness of this world, against spiritual wickedness in high places. Wherefore take unto you the whole armor of God, that ye may be able to withstand in the evil day, and having done all, to stand. Stand therefore, having your loins girt about with truth and having on the breastplate of righteousness; and your feet shod with the preparation of the gospel of peace; above all, taking the shield of faith, wherewith ye shall be able to quench all the fiery darts of the wicked. And take the helmet of salvation, and the sword of the Spirit, which is the word of God: praying always with all prayer and supplication for all saints; and for me, that utterance may be given unto me, that I may open my mouth boldly, to make known the mystery of the gospel, for which I am ambassador in bonds: that therein I may speak boldly, as I ought to speak.

Amen, So it shall be. This is the spirit of David the anointed servant of God speaking through the spirit of the living God in Paul the New Testament teacher and preacher of righteousness.

The risen lord, manifesting the resurrection power of the triumphant victory over the grave, over principalities and power and wicked spirits in heavenly places. Death swallowed up great spoil. No God like Jehovah demonstrated in this combat of all combats. A perfect heavenly show. God led captivity captive. The devil no match for God of the Trinity. Hallelujah. That is what God is revealing to me about Psalm Ninety-One in terms of the new birth and the resurrection power. Hallelujah!

I have the rare privilege of reading that Psalm over hundreds of times many times each year. I read it at the end of each year minimum of ninety-one times each year;

I have the privilege of praying and reading it out loud for my family members for their number of their years;

In many of my hospital visitations to pray for the sick, I often prayed that psalm;

In my numerous travels all round the world, I never flew without praying for God's protection with Psalm 91

Before I drove my car when I left my home, I prayed Psalm 91.

When I traveled and rented a car, I prayed Psalm 91

Before a doctors visit, I prayed Psalm 91

When people are sick and dying, I prayed Psalm 91

I take daily Communion. I prayed Psalm 103, 23 and 91
When I was persecuted and lied against by a Muslim family, and was jailed here in Boston unjustly with no one evidence, I prayed Psalm 91 many times over in Framingham and over 400 women were saved. It hurt so much to suffer unjust for something that never happened but through the mighty resurrection power I was able to overcome with great joy through the power in the spoken word. There is power mighty in the Word of God. Psalm 91 was my staying power in the Blood of Jesus. In jail I prayed so many

times for so many prisoners and for myself, countless of times. Praise God!

I have the privilege of praying and reading it for many of my friends and Church members each year.

I have the privilege of praying it no less on the average a minimum of 15 times daily;

I have the privilege of praying it for myself on each birthday, and this year will be minimum eighty times. Hallelujah! Amen!

Bro Hagin has a book on The God who is more than enough. The El Shaddai. Truly God is more than Enough and that is why I believe we can say that Psalm 91 can be said to be a summary of the Bible because it represents the good news of the Bible.

I am so thankful that God has revealed and unveiled His redemptive name through, the sacrifice, self-emptying, life, death. Resurrection ascension, Pentecost and continues to showcase himself through His body, The Church. He is the Resurrection and Life. It is in Him, we live and move and have our being, the eternal life. He is the hope of the world. He is truly the one who is more than enough. He is the breasty one.

He dwells in the secret place of the most high, yet He is ever present help in time of trouble. He was never created yet He created everything. He is my God, my all in all.

Recently my kid brother had a major, seven hours of impossible disc surgery in Lagos, Nigeria. I prayed Psalm 91, hundreds of times in two days and God gave me such peace that He answered our prayer before we saw the manifestation. I knew in my spirit that God will come through for us. Not by power, not by might, but only by the Spirit of the living God. Amen!

In the last few years, starting with the end of 2018 we encountered man me plague that went from Wuhan, China making its way to the USA and so many countries. Going back we had the Egyptian plagues as a result of disobedience in oppressing the Children of Israel. Please read the book of Exodus to read the account of this. The plagues can be found fully from Exodus 5-11. Bro Hagin mentioned of a bubonic plague that happened about 1970 (see Health Food Devotions, March 16-17 and how Congregational Pastor, Rev Dowie interceded and God intervened and stopped the death that was ravaging his congregation after he found out that devil, not God was responsible for the bubonic devastation. God gave him Acts 10:38 and the spirit of death was pushed back in the twinkle of an eye.

The 2019 Covid was from the pit of hell and God, who is rich in mercy was not responsible for any sickness and disease. Every sickness and disease that is in the world is from the pit of hell. I praise God, that no sickness come from heaven. Satan is the author of sickness and death. Even Christians who do not read the Bible accuse God of evil. The fact that so called Christians accuse God evil is obvious that they do not spend time reading the Word of God or are deceived into believing the lie of the evil one.

I stand on the Word of God that no evil shall come near my dwelling. Sickness and disease cannot survive in my body because "greater is God that is in me than he that it is in the world" (1 John 4:4b), because Jesus won the victory on the cross of Calvary. Amen

Joy is His nature and at the same time, He brings great comfort in time of sorrow. Hallelujah!!! Praise the Lord.

It is the Lord's doing that I am able to put this today. It is an original because as far as I know, this is the project of this kind of Psalm 91. I had the only car in New England with Psalm 91. I sold my brand new car just before the pandemic. I had that Plate Number for about two decades. People have stopped me in the streets of Boston to recite and pray that psalm for them. Thank you Jesus for your love, mercy and protection! Amen!

As Psalm 91:2 - I will say of the Lord, He is my refuge and my fortress, my God in him will I trust. Amen!

When I pray it, I say, You are my refuge and my fortress, my God in You I trust continuously. I am in Christ already, therefore I chose to trust God my Lord and Savior at all times because He is faithful and just. Our God is a good God at all times. Amen! His nature is love, goodness, mercy, full of compassion.

Psalm 91 Amplified Bible

Security of the One Who Trusts in the LORD.

91 He who [a]dwells in the shelter of the Most High
Will remain secure and rest in the shadow of the Almighty
[whose power no enemy can withstand].

2 I will say of the LORD, "He is my refuge and my fortress,
My God, in whom I trust [with great confidence, and on whom I
rely]!"

3 For He will save you from the trap of the fowler,
And from the deadly pestilence.

4 He will cover you *and* completely protect you with His pinions, And
under His wings you will find refuge;
His faithfulness is a shield and a wall.

5 You will not be afraid of the terror of night,
Nor of the arrow that flies by day,

6 Nor of the pestilence that stalks in darkness,
Nor of the destruction (sudden death) that lays waste at noon.

7 A thousand may fall at your side
And ten thousand at your right hand,
But danger will not come near you.

8 You will only [be a spectator as you] look on with your eyes And
witness the [divine] repayment of the wicked [as you watch safely
from the shelter of the Most High].

9 Because you have made the LORD, [who is] my refuge,
Even the Most High, your dwelling place,

10   No evil will befall you,
Nor will any plague come near your tent.

11   For He will command His angels in regard to you,
To protect and defend and guard you in all your ways [of obedience and service]

12   They will lift you up in their hands,
So that you do not [even] strike your foot against a stone.

13   You will tread upon the lion and cobra;
The young lion and the serpent you will trample underfoot.

14   "Because he set his love on Me, therefore I will save him;
I will set him [securely] on high, because he knows My name [he confidently trusts and relies on Me, knowing I will never abandon him, no, never].

15   "He will call upon Me, and I will answer him;
I will be with him in trouble;
I will rescue him and honor him.

16   "With a long life I will satisfy him
And I will let him see My salvation."

Footnotes

a. Psalm 91:1 The wonderful promises of this chapter are dependent upon one's meeting the conditions stated in these first two verses (see Ex)

Psalm 91 1599 Geneva Bible

91 *1 Here is described in what assurance he liveth, that putteth his whole trust in God, and commiteth himself wholly to his protection in all temptations. 14 A promise of God to those that love him, knowhim, and trust in him to deliver them, and give them immortal glory.*

¹ Who so dwelleth in the [a]secret of the most High, shall abide in the shadow of the Almighty.

² [b]I will say unto the Lord, O my hope, and my fortress: *he is* my God, in him will I trust.

³ Surely I will deliver thee from the [c]snare of the hunter, *and* from the noisome pestilence.

⁴ He will cover thee under his wings, and thou shalt be sure under his feathers: his [dtruth shall be thy shield and buckler.

⁵ [e] Thou shalt not be afraid of the fear of the night: *nor* of the arrow that flieth by day:

⁶ *Nor* of the pestilence that walketh in the darkness: *nor* of the plague that destroyeth at noon day.

⁷ A thousand shall fall at thy side, and ten thousand at thy right hand, *but* it shall not come near thee.

⁸ Doubtless with thine [f]eyes shalt thou behold and see the reward of the wicked.

⁹ For thou *hast* said, The Lord *is* mine hope: thou hast set the most High for thy refuge.

¹⁰ There shall none evil come unto thee, neither shall any plague come near thy tabernacle.

¹¹ [g]For he shall give his Angels charge over thee to keep thee in all thy ways.

¹² They shall bear thee in their hands, that thou hurt not thy foot against a stone.

¹³ Thou shalt walk upon the lion and asp: the [h]young lion, and the dragon shalt thou tread under feet.

¹⁴ [i]Because he hath loved me, therefore will I deliver him: I will exalt him because he hath known my Name.

¹⁵ He shall call upon me, and I will hear him: I will be with him in trouble: I will deliver him, and glorify him.

¹⁶ With [j]long life will I satisfy him, and show him my salvation.

Footnotes

a. Psalm 91:1 He that maketh God his defense and trust, shall perceive his protection to be a most sure safeguard.

b. Psalm 91:2 Being assured of this protection, he prayeth unto the Lord.

c. Psalm 91:3 That is, God's help is most ready for us, whether Satan assail us secretly, which he calleth a snare: or openly, which is here meant by the pestilence.

d. Psalm 91:4 That is, his faithful keeping of promise to help thee in thy necessity.

e. Psalm 91:5 The care that God hath over his, is most sufficient to defend them from all dangers.

f. Psalm 91:8 The godly shall have some experience of God's judgments against the wicked even in this life, but fully they shall see it at that day when all things shall be revealed.

g. Psalm 91:11 God hath not appointed every man one Angel, but many to be ministers of his providence to keep his, and defend them in their vocation, which is the way to walk in without tempting God.

h. Psalm 91:13 Thou shalt not only be preserved from all evil, but overcome it whether it be secret or open.

i. Psalm 91:14 To assure the faithful of God's protection, he bringeth in God to confirm the same.

j. Psalm 91:16 For he is contented with that life that God giveth: for by death the shortness of this life is recompensed with immortality.

Psalm 91 Holman Christian Standard Bible

Psalm 91

The Protection of the Most High

1   The one who lives under the protection of the Most High dwells in
the shadow of the Almighty.

2   I will say[a] to the LORD, "My refuge and my fortress,
my God, in whom I trust."

3   He Himself will deliver you from the hunter's net,
from the destructive plague.

4   He will cover you with His feathers;
you will take refuge under His wings.
His faithfulness will be a protective shield.

5   You will not fear the terror of the night,
the arrow that flies by day,

6   the plague that stalks in darkness,
or the pestilence that ravages at noon.

7   and ten thousand at your right hand,
Though a thousand fall at your side
the pestilence will not reach you.

8   You will only see it with your eyes
and witness the punishment of the wicked.

9   Because you have made the LORD-my refuge,
the Most High-your dwelling place,

10   no harm will come to you;
      no plague will come near your tent.

11   For He will give His angels orders concerning you,
      to protect you in all your ways.

12   They will support you with their hands
      so that you will not strike your foot against a stone.

13   You will tread on the lion and the cobra;
      you will trample the young lion and the serpent.

14   Because he is lovingly devoted to Me,
      I will deliver him;
      I will protect him because he knows My name.

15   When he calls out to Me, I will answer him;
      I will be with him in trouble.
      I will rescue him and give him honor.

16   I will satisfy him with a long life
      and show him My salvation.

Footnotes

a. Psalm 91:2 LXX, Syr, Jer read ² Almighty, saying, or ² Almighty, he will say

Psalm 91 New Living Translation

Psalm 91

1   Those who live in the shelter of the Most High
     will find rest in the shadow of the Almighty.

2   This I declare about the LORD:
     He alone is my refuge, my place of safety;
     he is my God, and I trust him.

3   For he will rescue you from every trap
     and protect you from deadly disease.

4   He will cover you with his feathers.
     He will shelter you with his wings.
     His faithful promises are your armor and protection.

5   Do not be afraid of the terrors of the night,
     nor the arrow that flies in the day.

6   Do not dread the disease that stalks in darkness,
     nor the disaster that strikes at midday.

7   Though a thousand fall at your side,
     though ten thousand are dying around you,
     these evils will not touch you.

8   Just open your eyes,
     and see how the wicked are punished.

9   If you make the LORD your refuge,
     if you make the Most High your shelter,

10   no evil will conquer you;
     no plague will come near your home.

11   For he will order his angels
     to protect you wherever you go.

12   They will hold you up with their hands

       so you won't even hurt your foot on a stone.

13   You will trample upon lions and cobras;

       you will crush fierce lions and serpents under your feet!

14   The LORD says, "I will rescue those who love me.

       I will protect those who trust in my name.

15   When they call on me,

       I will answer;

       I will be with them in trouble.

16   I will reward them with a long life

       and give them my salvation."

Psalm 91 The Message

91   **1-13** You who sit down in the High God's presence,
　　　spend the night in Shaddai's shadow,
Say this: "GOD, you're my refuge.
　　I trust in you and I'm safe!"
That's right-he rescues you from hidden traps,
　shields you from deadly hazards.
His huge outstretched arms protect you-
　　under them you're perfectly safe;
　　his arms fend off all harm.
Fear nothing-not wild wolves in the night,
　　not flying arrows in the day,
Not disease that prowls through the darkness,
　　not disaster that erupts at high noon.
Even though others   succumb all around,
　　drop like flies right and left,
　　no harm will even graze you.
You'll stand untouched, watch it all from a distance,
　　watch the wicked turn into corpses.
Yes, because GOD's your refuge,
　　the High God your very own home,
Evil can't get close to you,
　harm can't get through the door.
He ordered his angels
　　to guard you wherever you go.
If you stumble, they'll catch you;
　　their job is to keep you from falling.
You'll walk unharmed among lions and snakes,
　　and kick young lions and serpents from the path.

14-16 "If you'll hold on to me for dear life," says GOD,
    "I'll get you out of any trouble.
I'll give you the best of care
    if you'll only get to know and trust me.
Call me and I'll answer, be at your side in bad times;
    I'll rescue you, then throw you a party.
I'll give you a long life,
    give you a long drink of salvation!"

Psalm 91 King James Version

91 He that dwelleth in the secret place of the most
High shall abide under the shadow of the Almighty.

2 I will say of the LORD, He is my refuge and my fortress: my God;
in him will I trust.

3 Surely he shall deliver thee from the snare of the fowler, and from
the noisome pestilence.

4 He shall cover thee with his feathers, and under his wings shalt thou
trust: his truth shall be thy shield and buckler.

5 Thou shalt not be afraid for the terror by night; nor for the arrow
that flieth by day;

6 Nor for the pestilence that walketh in darkness; nor for the
destruction that wasteth at noonday.

7 *Nor* of the pestilence that walketh in the darkness: *nor* of the plague
that destroyeth at noon day.

8 A thousand shall fall at thy side, and ten thousand at thy right hand;
but it shall not come nigh thee.

9 Only with thine eyes shalt thou behold and see the reward of the
wicked.

10 A There shall no evil befall thee, neither shall any plague come nigh
thy dwelling.

11 For he shall give his angels charge over thee, to keep thee in all thy
ways.

12 They shall bear thee up in their hands, lest thou dash thy foot
against a stone

13 Thou shalt tread upon the iron and adder: the young lion and the dragon shalt thou trample under feet.

14 Because he hath set his love upon me, therefore will I deliver him: I will set him on high, because he hath known my name.

15 He shall call upon me, and I will answer him: I will be with him in trouble; I will deliver him and honour him.

16 With long life I will satisfy him, and shew him my salvation.

Psalm 91
Nouvelle Edition de Genève - NEG1979

Protection toute suffisante de Dieu

91 Celui qui demeure sous l'abri du Très- Haut
Repose à l'ombre du Tout-Puissant.

2 Je dis à l'Eternel: Mon refuge et ma forteresse,
Mon Dieu en qui je me confie!

3 Car c'est lui qui te délivre du filet de l'oiseleur,
De la peste et de ses ravages.

4 Il te couvrira de ses plumes,
Et tu trouveras un refuge sous ses ailes; Sa fidélité est un bouclier et une cuirasse.

5 Tu ne craindras ni les terreurs de la nuit,
Ni la flèche qui vole de jour,

6 Ni la peste qui marche dans les ténèbres,
Ni la contagion qui frappe en plein midi.

7 Que mille tombent à ton côté,
Et dix mille à ta droite,
Tu ne seras pas atteint;

8 De tes yeux seulement tu regarderas,
Et tu verras la rétribution des méchants.

9 Car tu es mon refuge, ô Eternel!
Tu fais du Très-Haut ta retraite.

10 Aucun malheur ne t'arrivera,
Aucun fléau n'approchera de ta tente.

11 Car il ordonnera à ses anges
De te garder dans toutes tes voies;

12 Ils te porteront sur les mains,
De peur que ton pied ne heurte contre une pierre[a].

13	Tu marcheras sur le lion et sur l'aspic,
	Tu fouleras le lionceau et le dragon.
14	Puisqu'il m'aime, je le délivrerai;
	Je le protégerai, puisqu'il connaît mon nom.
15	Il m'invoquera, et je lui répondrai;
	Je serai avec lui dans la détresse,
	Je le délivrerai et je le glorifierai.
16	Je le rassasierai de longs jours,
	Et je lui ferai voir mon salut.

Footnotes

a. Psaumes 91:12 + Mt 4:6; + Lu 4:10, 11

Psalm 91
New International Version

Psalm 91

1   Whoever dwells in the shelter of the Most High
will rest in the shadow of the Almighty.[a]

2   I will say of the LORD, "He is my refuge and my fortress,
my God, in whom I trust."

3   Surely he will save you
from the fowler's snare
and from the deadly pestilence.

4   He will cover you with his feathers,
and under his wings you will find refuge;
his faithfulness will be your shield and rampart.

5   You will not fear the
terror of night, nor the arrow that flies by day,

6   nor the pestilence that stalks in the darkness,
nor the plague that destroys at midday.

7   A thousand may fall at your side,
ten thousand at your right hand, but it will not come near
you.

8   You will only observe with your eyes
and see the punishment of the wicked.

9   If you say, 'The LORD
is my refuge," and you make the Most High your
dwelling,

10   no harm will overtake you,
no disaster will come near your tent.

11   For he will command his angels concerning you
to guard you in all your ways;

12   they will lift you up in their hands,
         so that you will not strike your foot against a stone.

13   You will tread on the lion and the cobra; you will trample
         the great lion and the serpent.

14   "Because he[b] loves me," says the LORD, "I will rescue him;
         I will protect him, for he acknowledges my name.

15   He will call on me, and I will answer him; I will be with him
         in trouble,
         I will deliver him and honor him.

16   With long life I will satisfy him
         and show him my salvation."

Footnotes

a. Psalm 91:1 Hebrew Shaddai
b. Psalm 91:14 That is probably the king

Psalm 91 Darby Translation

91 He that dwelleth in the secret place of the Most High shall abide under the shadow of the Almighty.

2 I say of Jehovah, My refuge and my fortress; my God, I will confide in him.

3 Surely *he* shall deliver thee from the snare of the fowler, [and] from the destructive pestilence.

4 He shall cover thee with his feathers, and under his wings shalt thou find refuge: his truth is a shield and buckler.

5 Thou shalt not be afraid for the terror by night, for the arrow that flieth by day,

6 For the pestilence that walketh in darkness, for the destruction that wasteth at noonday.

7 A thousand shall fall at thy side, and ten thousand at thy right hand; [but] it shall not come nigh thee.

8 Only with thine eyes shalt thou behold, and see the reward of the wicked.

9 Because "thou* hast made Jehovah, my refuge, the Most High, thy dwelling-place,

10 There shall no evil befall thee, neither shall any plague come nigh thy tent.

11 For he shall give his angels charge concerning thee, to keep thee in all thy ways:

12 They shall bear thee up in [their] hands, lest thou dash thy foot against a stone.

13 Thou shalt tread upon the lion and the adder; the young lion and the dragon shalt thou trample under foot.

14 Because he hath set his love upon me, therefore will I deliver him; I will set him on high, because he hath known my name.

15 He shall call upon me, and I will answer him; I will be with him in trouble, I will deliver him and honour him.

16 With length of days will I satisfy him, and shew him my salvation.

Psalm 91 Complete Jewish Bible

91   You who live in the shelter of 'Elyon,
       who spend your nights in the shadow of Shaddai,

2   who say to ADONAI, "My refuge! My fortress!
       My God, in whom I trust!"

3   he will rescue you from the trap of the hunter
       and from the plague of calamities;

4   he will cover you with his pinions,
       and under his wings you will find refuge;
       his truth is a shield and protection.

5   You will not fear the terrors of night
       or the arrow that flies by day,

6   or the plague that roams in the dark,
       or the scourge that wreaks havoc at noon

7   A thousand may fall at your side,
       ten thousand at your right hand;
       but it won't come near you.

8   Only keep your eyes open,
       and you will see how the wicked are punished.

9   For you have made ADONAI, the Most High,
       who is my refuge, your dwelling-place.

10   No disaster will happen to you,
       no calamity will come near your tent;

11   for he will order his angels to care for you
       and guard you wherever you go.

12   They will carry you in their hands,
       so that you won't trip on a stone.

13   You will tread down lions and snakes,
       young lions and serpents you will trample underfoot.

14   "Because he loves me, I will rescue him;
       because he knows my name, I will protect him.

15   He will call on me, and I will answer him.
       I will be with him when he is in trouble.
       I will extricate him and bring him honor.

16   I will satisfy him with long life
       and show him my salvation."

Psalm 91 American Standard Version

Security of him who trusts in Jehovah.

91 He that dwelleth in the secret place of the Most High
[a]Shall abide under the shadow of the Almighty.

2 I will say of Jehovah, He is my refuge and my fortress;
My God, in whom I trust.

3 For he will deliver thee from the snare of the fowler,
And from the deadly pestilence.

4 He will cover thee with his pinions,
And under his wings shalt thou take refuge:
His truth is a shield and a buckler.

5 Thou shalt not be afraid for the terror by night,
Nor for the arrow that flieth by day;

6 For the pestilence that walketh in darkness,
Nor for the destruction that wasteth at noonday.

7 A thousand shall fall at thy side,
And ten thousand at thy right hand;
But it shall not come nigh thee.

8 Only with thine eyes shalt thou behold,
And see the reward of the wicked.

9 [b]For thou, O Jehovah, art my refuge!
Thou hast made the Most High thy habitation;

10 There shall no evil befall thee,
Neither shall any plague come nigh thy tent.

11 For he will give his angels charge over thee,
To keep thee in all thy ways.

12 They shall bear thee up in their hands,
Lest thou dash thy foot against a stone.

13 Thou shalt tread upon the lion and adder:
The young lion and the serpent shalt thou trample under foot.

14 Because he hath set his love upon me, therefore will I deliver him:
I will set him on high, because he hath known my name.
He shall call upon me, and I will answer him;

15 He shall call upon me, and I will answer him;
I will be with him in trouble:
I will deliver him, and honor him.

16 With long life will I satisfy him, And show him my salvation.

Psalm 91 BRG Bible

Psalm 91

¹ He that dwelleth in the secret place of the most High shall abide under the shadow of the Almighty.

² I will say of the LORD, He is my refuge and my fortress: my God; in him will I trust.

³ Surely he shall deliver thee from the snare of the fowler, and from the noisome pestilence.

⁴ He shall cover thee with his feathers, and under his wings shalt thou trust: his truth shall be thy shield and buckler.

⁵ Thou shalt not be afraid for the terror by night; nor for the arrow that flieth by day;

⁶ Nor for the pestilence that walketh in darkness; nor for the destruction that wasteth at noonday.

⁷ A thousand shall fall at thy side, and ten thousand at thy right hand; but it shall not come nigh thee.

⁸ Only with thine eyes shalt thou behold and see the reward of the wicked.

⁹ Because thou hast made the LORD, which is my refuge, even the most High, thy habitation;

¹⁰ There shall no evil befall thee, neither shall any plague come nigh thy dwelling.

¹¹ For he shall give his angels charge over thee, to keep thee in all thy ways.

¹² They shall bear thee up in their hands, lest thou dash thy foot against a stone.

¹³ Thou shalt tread upon the lion and adder: the young lion and the dragon shalt thou trample under feet.

¹⁴ Because he hath set his love upon me, therefore will I deliver him: I will set him on high, because he hath known my name.

¹⁵ He shall call upon me, and I will answer him: I will be with him in trouble; I will deliver him, and honour him.

¹⁶ With long life will I satisfy him, and shew him my salvation.

91 De, der søger hjælp hos den Højeste,
bliver beskyttet af den almægtige Gud.

2 Jeg siger til Herren: „Du er min tilflugt,
jeg stoler trygt på dig, min Gud."

3 Han bevarer dig fra at gå i fælden,
redder dig fra dødelige sygdomme.

4 Han dækker dig med sine fjer,
du er tryg under hans vinger.
Du kan fuldt ud stole på hans hjælp.

5 Du skal ikke ligge vågen om natten af frygt,
eller være bange for de pile, der flyver om dagen.

6 Du skal ikke ængstes for at blive syg om natten,
eller for at ulykker skal ramme dig ved højlys dag.

7 Om så tusinde falder ved siden af dig,
eller ti tusinde bukker under omkring dig,
skal ulykken ikke ramme dig.

8 Med dine egne øjne får du at se,
hvordan gudløse mennesker bliver straffet.

9 Når du søger tilflugt hos Herren,
og beder den Almægtige beskytte dig,

10 skal du ikke rammes af noget ondt,
ingen ulykke skal ødelægge dit hjem.

11 For han befaler sine engle at passe på dig,
de skal vogte dig, hvor du end går.

12 De skal bære dig på hænder,
så du ikke støder din fod på nogen sten.

13 Du kan overvinde både løver og slanger
og sætte din fod på dem som sejrherre.

14 Herren siger: „Jeg redder dem, der elsker mig,
beskytter dem, der har tillid til mig.

15 Når de kalder, vil jeg svare.
Jeg hjælper dem, når de har problemer,
redder dem og giver dem oprejsning.

16 Jeg velsigner dem med et langt liv,
de skal opleve, at jeg frelser dem."

Salme 91 Luther Bibel 1545

91 Wer unter dem Schirm des Höchsten sitzt und unter dem Schatten des Allmächtigen bleibt,

2 der spricht zu dem HERRN: Meine Zuversicht und meine Burg, mein Gott, auf den ich hoffe.

3 Denn er errettet dich vom Strick des Jägers und von der schädlichen Pestilenz.

4 Er wird dich mit seinen Fittichen decken, und deine Zuversicht wird sein unter seinen Flügeln. Seine Wahrheit ist Schirm und Schild,

5 daß du nicht erschrecken müssest vor dem Grauen der Nacht, vor den Pfeilen, die des Tages fliegen,

6 vor der Pestilenz, die im Finstern schleicht, vor der Seuche, die im Mittage verderbt.

7 Ob tausend fallen zu deiner Seite und zehntausend zu deiner Rechten, so wird es doch dich nicht treffen.

8 Ja du wirst mit deinen Augen deine Lust sehen und schauen, wie den Gottlosen vergolten wird.

9 Denn der HERR ist deine Zuversicht; der Höchste ist deine Zuflucht.

10 Es wird dir kein Übel begegnen, und keine Plage wird zu deiner Hütte sich nahen

11 Denn er hat seinen Engeln befohlen über dir, daß sie dich behüten auf allen deinen Wegen,

¹² daß sie dich auf Händen tragen und du deinen Fuß nicht an einen Stein stoßest.

¹³ Auf Löwen und Ottern wirst du gehen, und treten auf junge Löwen und Drachen.

¹⁴ "Er begehrt mein, so will ich ihm aushelfen; er kennt meinen Namen, darum will ich ihn schützen.

¹⁵ Er ruft mich an, so will ich ihn erhören; ich bin bei ihm in der Not; ich will ihn herausreißen und zu Ehren bringen.

¹⁶ 16 Ich will ihn sättigen mit langem Leben und will ihm zeigen mein Heil."

Psalm 91 Names of God Bible

Psalm 91

1   Whoever lives under the shelter of Elyon

    will remain in the shadow of Shadday.

2   I will say to **Yahweh**,

    "You are my **Machseh** and my **Metsuda**, my **Elohim** in whom I

trust."

3   He is the one who will rescue you from hunters' traps

    and from deadly plagues.

4   He will cover you with his feathers,

    and under his wings you will find refuge.

      His truth is your shield and armor.

5   You do not need to fear

    terrors of the night,

      arrows that fly during the day,

6   plagues that roam the dark,

    epidemics that strike at noon.

7   They will not come near you,

    even though a thousand may fall dead beside you

      or ten thousand at your right side.

8   You only have to look with your eyes

    to see the punishment of wicked people.

9   You, O **Yahweh**, are my **Machseh**!

    You have made **Elyon** your home.

10   No harm will come to you.

    No sickness will come near your house

11   He will put his angels in charge of you

      to protect you in all your ways.

12   They will carry you in their hands

      so that you never hit your foot against a rock.

13   You will step on lions and cobras.

      You will trample young lions and snakes.

14   Because you love me, I will rescue you.

      I will protect you because you know my name.

15   When you call to me, I will answer you.

      I will be with you when you are in trouble.

        I will save you and honor you.

16   I will satisfy you with a long life.

      I will show you how I will save you.

Psalm 91 Young's Literal Translation

91 He who is dwelling In the secret place of the Most High, In the shade of the Mighty lodgeth habitually,

2 He is saying of Jehovah, `My refuge, and my bulwark, my God, I trust in Him,'

3 For He delivereth thee from the snare of a fowler, From a calamitous pestilence.

4 With His pinion He covereth thee over, And under His wings thou dost trust, A shield and buckler [is] His truth.

5 Thou art not afraid of fear by night, Of arrow that flieth by day,

6 Of pestilence in thick darkness that walketh, Of destruction that destroyeth at noon,

7 There fall at thy side a thousand, And a myriad at thy right hand, Unto thee it cometh not nigh.

8 But with thine eyes thou lookest, And the reward of the wicked thou seest,

9 (For Thou, O Jehovah, [art] my refuge,) The Most High thou madest thy habitation.

10 Evil happeneth not unto thee, And a plague cometh not near thy tent,

11 For His messengers He chargeth for thee, To keep thee in all thy ways,

12 On the hands they bear thee up, Lest thou smite against a stone thy foot,

13 On lion and asp thou treadest, Thou trampest young lion and dragon.

14 Because in Me he hath delighted, I also deliver him -- I set him on high, Because he hath known My name.

15 He doth call Me, and I answer him, I [am] with him in distress, I deliver him, and honour him.

16 With length of days I satisfy him, And I cause him to look on My salvation!

91 He that dwelleth in the seter Elyon (covering, hiding place of the Most High) shall abide under the tzel Shaddai (shadow of the Almighty).

² I will say of Hashem, He is my refuge and my fortress; Elohai (my G-d); in Him will I trust.

³ Surely He shall save thee from the pach yakosh ([deadly] snare of the fowler), and from the devastating dever (plague).

⁴ He shall cover thee with His evrah (pinion, flight feathers), and under His kenafayim (wings) shalt thou find defense; His Emes shall be thy shield and buckler.

⁵ Thou shalt not be afraid of the pachad (terror) by lailah; nor of the khetz (arrow) that flieth yomam (by day);

⁶ Nor for the dever (plague) that walketh in darkness; nor for the ketev (pestilence, destruction) that destroyeth at tzohorayim (noon).

⁷ An elef (thousand) may fall at thy side, and ten thousand at thy yamin (right hand); but it shall not come near thee.

⁸ Only with thine eyes shalt thou behold and see the shillumah (recompense, retribution) of the resha'im.

⁹ Because thou hast made Hashem, which is my refuge, even Elyon, thy ma'on (habitation, dwelling; see _Yn 14:2_ OJBC)

¹⁰ There shall no ra'ah (evil, disaster) befall thee, neither shall any nega come near thy ohel.

¹¹ For He shall give charge to His malachim (angels) concerning thee, to be shomer over thee in kol drakhim of thee.

12 They [the malachim of Hashem] shall bear thee up on their palms, lest thou dash thy regel against an even (stone).

13 Thou shalt tread upon the lion and adder; the young lion and the tannin (serpent) shalt thou trample under foot.

14 Because he hath set his longing upon Me, therefore will I rescue him; I will set him on high, because he hath da'as of Shmi (My Name).

15 He shall call upon Me, and I will answer him; I will be with him in tzoros; I will deliver him, and honor him.

16 With orech yamim (length of days, long life) will I satisfy him, and show him My Yeshuah (salvation).

Psalm 91 The Voice

Psalm 91

1   He who takes refuge in the shelter of the Most High
      will be safe in the shadow of the Almighty.

2   He will say to the Eternal, "My shelter, my mighty fortress,
      my God, I place all my trust in You."

3   For He will rescue you from the snares set by your enemies who
      entrap you and from deadly plagues.

4   Like a bird protecting its young, God will cover you with His feathers,
      will protect you under His great wings;
      His faithfulness will form a shield around you, a rock-solid wall to
      protect

Psalm 91 is a beautiful psalm of trust in God. But how does God take
care of all His people, all at the same time? Well, keep reading because
Psalm 91 is one of just a few places in Scripture that describe what we
might call "guardian angels" (Exodus 23:20; Psalm 43:3). Though rare,
these passages teach that God is not alone in maintaining and protecting
His creation and His people. He has made a host of heavenly messengers
ready to do His bidding, and His bidding is often to guard His people
throughout their lives and protect them-sometimes from dangers
they are not even aware of.

5   You will not dread the terrors that haunt the night
      or enemy arrows that fly in the day

6   Or the plagues that lurk in darkness
      or the disasters that wreak havoc at noon.

7   A thousand may fall on your left,

ten thousand may die on your right,

but these horrors won't come near you.

8   Only your eyes will witness

the punishment that awaits the evil,

but you will not suffer because of it.

9   For you made the Eternal [your] [a] refuge,

the Most High your only home.

10   No evil will come to you;

plagues will be turned away at your door.

11   He will command His heavenly messengers to guard you,

to keep you safe in every way.

12   They will hold you up in their hands

so that you will not crash, or fall, or even graze your foot on a stone.[b]

13   You will walk on the lion and the cobra;

you will trample the lion and the serpent underfoot.

14   "Because he clings to Me in love,

I will rescue him from harm;

I will set him above danger.

15   When you call to me, I will answer you.

I will be with you when you are in trouble.

I will save you and honor you.

Because he has known Me by name,

16   I'll reward him with many good years on this earth

and let him witness My salvation."

Footnotes

a. 91:9 Hebrew manuscripts read, "who is my."

b. 91:11-12 Matthew 4:6; Luke 4:10-11

Psalm 91 nuBibeln (Swedish Contemporary Bible)

Guds beskydd i farans stund

91 Den som bor i den Högstes skydd

och vilar i den Väldiges skugga,

2 han[a] säger: "HERREN är min tillflykt och min borg,

min Gud, som jag förtröstar på."

3 Han räddar dig från jägarens snara

och från dödlig pest.

4 Med sina vingar täcker han dig,

under dem finner du tillflykt.

Hans trofasthet är en sköld och en skyddsmur.

5 Du behöver inte vara rädd för nattens fasor

eller för pilen som flyger på dagen,

6 inte pesten som går fram i mörkret

eller plågan som härjar mitt på dagen.

7 Även om tusen faller vid din sida,

tiotusen till höger om dig,

drabbas inte du.

8 Med egna ögon ska du få se på

hur de gudlösa straffas.

9 För du har gjort HERREN till din tillflykt,

den Högste till ditt beskydd.

10 Inget ont ska hända dig

och ingen olycka komma nära ditt tält.

11 Han ger sina änglar befallning

om att skydda dig var du än går.

12   Med sina händer ska de bära dig,

       så att du inte stöter din fot mot någon sten.

13   Över unga lejon och kobror går du fram,

       du trampar på vilddjur och ormar.

14   "Eftersom han älskar mig,

       ska jag rädda honom.

       Jag ska skydda honom,

       eftersom han känner mitt namn.

15   När han ropar på mig,

       ska jag svara honom.

       Jag ska vara med honom i nöden,

       rädda honom och ge honom ära.

16   Jag ska mätta honom med ett långt liv

       och låta honom se den räddning jag ger."

Footnotes

a. 91:2 Egentligen jag; här följer översättningen Septuaginta m.fl.

91 Sæll er sá, er situr í skjóli Hins hæsta, sá er gistir í skugga Hins almáttka,

[2] sá er segir við Drottin: "Hæli mitt og háborg, Guð minn, er ég trúi á!"

[3] Hann frelsar þig úr snöru fuglarans, frá drepsótt glötunarinnar,

[4] hann skýlir þér með fjöðrum sínum, undir vængjum hans mátt þú hælis leita, trúfesti hans er skjöldur og verja.

[5] Eigi þarft þú að óttast ógnir næturinnar, eða örina, sem flýgur um daga,

[6] drepsóttina, er reikar um í dimmunni, eða sýkina, er geisar um hádegið.

[7] Þótt þúsund falli þér við hlið og tíu þúsund þér til hægri handar, þá nær það ekki til þín.

[8] Þú horfir aðeins á með augunum, sér hversu óguðlegum er endurgoldið.

[9] Þitt hæli er Drottinn, þú hefir gjört Hinn hæsta að athvarfi þínu.

[10] Engin ógæfa hendir þig, og engin plága nálgast tjald þitt.

[11] því að þín vegna býður hann út englum sínum til þess að gæta þín á öllum vegum þínum.

[12] þeir munu bera þig á höndum sér, til þess að þú steytir ekki fót þinn við steini.

[13] Þú skalt stíga ofan á höggorma og nöðrur, troða fótum ljón og dreka.

[14] "Af því að hann leggur ást á mig, mun ég frelsa hann, ég bjarga honum, af því að hann þekkir nafn mitt.

[15] Ákalli hann mig, mun ég bænheyra hann, ég er hjá honum í neyðinni, ég frelsa hann og gjöri hann vegsamlegan.

[16] Ég metta hann með fjöld lífdaga og læt hann sjá hjálpræði mitt."

Psalm 91 New Century Version

Safe in the LORD

91 Those who go to God Most High for safety

will be protected by the Almighty.

2 I will say to the LORD, "You are my place of safety and protection.

You are my God and I trust you."

3 God will save you from hidden traps

and from deadly diseases.

4 He will cover you with his feathers,

and under his wings you can hide.

His truth will be your shield and protection.

5 You will not fear any danger by night

or an arrow during the day.

6 You will not be afraid of diseases that come in the dark

or sickness that strikes at noon.

7 At your side one thousand people may die,

or even ten thousand right beside you,

but you will not be hurt.

8 You will only watch

and see the wicked punished.

9 The LORD is your protection;

you have made God Most High your place of safety.

10 Nothing bad will happen to you;

no disaster will come to your home.

11 He has put his angels in charge of you

     to watch over you wherever you go.

12 They will catch you in their hands

     so that you will not hit your foot on a rock.

13 You will walk on lions and cobras;

     you will step on strong lions and snakes.

14 The LORD says, "Whoever loves me, I will save.

     I will protect those who know me.

15 They will call to me, and I will answer them.

     I will be with them in trouble;

     I will rescue them and honor them.

16 I will give them a long, full life,

     and they will see how I can save."

Sòm 91   Haitian Creole Version

91 Moun ki chache pwoteksyon bò kote Bondye ki anwo nan syèl la, moun ki rete kache anba zèl Bondye ki gen tout pouvwa a

2 ka di Seyè a: --Se ou ki tout defans mwen. Se ou ki tout pwoteksyon mwen. Ou se Bondye mwen. Se nan ou mwen mete tout konfyans mwen.

3 Se li menm ki p'ap kite ou pran nan pèlen, ki p'ap kite maladi ki pou touye ou tonbe sou ou.

4 L'ap kouvri ou anba zèl li. Anyen p'ap rive ou kote ou kache a. L'ap toujou kenbe pawòl li: Se sa ki pwoteksyon ou, se sa ki defans ou.

5 Ou pa bezwen pè bagay k'ap fè moun pè lannwit, ni kè ou pa bezwen kase pou malè ki ka rive ou lajounen.

6 Ou pa bezwen pè move maladi k'ap tonbe sou moun nan mitan lannwit, ni epidemi k'ap touye moun gwo midi.

7 Mil (1.000) moun te mèt tonbe sou bò gòch ou, dimil (10.000) sou bò dwat ou, anyen p'ap rive ou.

8 W'ap rete konsa, w'ap gade, w'a wè jan y'ap bay mechan yo sa yo merite.

9 Paske ou pran Seyè a pou defans ou, paske ou pran Bondye ki anwo nan syèl la pou pwoteksyon ou,

10 okenn malè p'ap rive ou, okenn mechan p'ap ka pwoche bò kot kay ou.

11 Bondye ap pase zanj li yo lòd pou yo veye sou ou, pou yo pwoteje ou kote ou pase.

12 Y'ap pote ou nan men yo. pou ou pa kase zòtèy pye ou sou okenn wòch.

¹³ W'ap mache sou lyon ak sou sèpan, w'ap kraze jenn ti lyon yo ak eskopyon yo anba pye ou.

¹⁴ Bondye di: M'ap sove moun ki renmen mwen, m'ap pwoteje moun ki konnen mwen.

¹⁵ Lè l' rele m', m'ap reponn li. Lè l' nan tray, m'ap la avèk li. M'ap delivre l', m'ap fè yo respekte l'.

¹⁶ M'ap fè l' viv lontan, m'a fè l' wè jan m'ap delivre l'.

91 Kan dega Ilaaha ugu sarreeya meeshiisa qarsoon
Wuxuu joogi doonaa hooska Qaadirka.

2 Waxaan Rabbiga ka odhan doonaa,
Isagu waa magangalkayga iyo qalcaddayda
Oo waa Ilaahayga aan isku halleeyo.

3 Waayo, wuxuu kaa samatabbixin doonaa dabinka ugaadhsadaha,
Iyo belaayada aad u xun.

4 Oo wuxuu kugu dedi doonaa baalashiisa,
Oo waxaad magangeli doontaa baadadkiisa,
Runtiisuna waxay tahay gaashaan iyo gabbaad.

5 Waa inaanad ka cabsan naxdinta habeennimada,
Iyo fallaadha dharaarnimada duulaysa toona,

6 Ama belaayada gudcurka ku socota,
Iyo halligaadda duhurka wax baabbi'isa

7 Dhinacaaga waxaa ku dhici doona kun,
Midigtaadana waxaa ku ag dhici doona toban kun,
Innabase kuuma soo dhowaan doonto.

8 Laakiinse indhaha uun baad ku fiirin doontaa,
Oo waxaad arki doontaa kuwa sharka leh abaalgudkooda.

9 Waayo, waxaad tidhi, Rabbigu waa magangalkayga,
Oo Kan ugu sarreeya ayaa degmadayda ah.

10 Shar kuguma dhici doono,
Belaayona teendhadaada uma soo dhowaan doonto.

11 Waayo, isagu wuxuu malaa'igihiisa ku amri doonaa
Inay jidadkaaga oo dhan kugu ilaaliyaan.

12 Oo iyaguna gacmahooday sare kuugu qaban doonaan
Inaanay cagtaadu dhagax ku dhicin.

13 Libaaxa iyo jilbiska ayaad ku joogsan doontaa,
Oo waxaad ku tuman doontaa aaran libaax iyo abeesada.

14 Rabbigu wuxuu yidhi, Isagu aad buu ii jeclaaday, oo sidaas
daraaddeed ayaan u samatabbixin doonaa,
Meel sare ayaan ku fadhiisin doonaa, maxaa yeelay, magacaygu
yiqiin.

¹⁵ Wuu i baryi doonaa, oo waan u jawaabi doonaa,
Oo markuu dhibaataysan yahay, waan la jiri doonaa,
Oo waan samatabbixin doonaa, waanan murwayn doonaa.

¹⁶ Cimri dheer ayaan ka dhergin doonaa,
Oo waxaan tusi doonaa badbaadintayda.

A segurança daquele que se refugia em Deus

91 Aquele que habita no esconderijo do Altíssimo, à sombra do Onipotente descansará. ² Direi do Senhor: Ele é o meu Deus, o meu refúgio, a minha fortaleza, e nele confiarei.

³ Porque ele te livrará do laço do passarinheiro e da peste perniciosa. ⁴ Ele te cobrirá com as suas penas, e debaixo das suas asas estarás seguro; a sua verdade é escudo e broquel. ⁵ Não temerás espanto noturno, nem seta que voe de dia, ⁶ nem peste que ande na escuridão, nem mortandade que assole ao meio-dia. ⁷ Mil cairão ao teu lado, e dez mil, à tua direita, mas tu não serás atingido. ⁸ Somente com os teus olhos olharás e verás a recompensa dos ímpios.

⁹ Porque tu, ó Senhor, és o meu refúgio! O Altíssimo é a tua habitação. ¹⁰ Nenhum mal te sucederá, nem praga alguma chegará à tua tenda. ¹¹ Porque aos seus anjos dará ordem a teu respeito, para te guardarem em todos os teus caminhos. ¹² Eles te sustentarão nas suas mãos, para que não tropeces com o teu pé em pedra. ¹³ Pisarás o leão e a áspide; calcarás aos pés o filho do leão e a serpente   .

¹⁴ Pois que tão encarecidamente me amou, também eu o livrarei; pô-lo-ei num alto retiro, porque conheceu o meu nome. ¹⁵ Ele me invocará, e eu lhe responderei; estarei com ele na angústia; livrá-lo-ei e o glorificarei. ¹⁶ Dar-lhe-ei abundância de dias e lhe mostrarei a minha salvação.

1 Onye nebi n'ebe-nzuzo nke Onye kachasi ihe nile elu,

O bu n'okpuru ǹdọ nke Onye puru ime ihe nile ka o nāno ọnọdu-abali.

2 M'gāsi Jehova, I bu ebe-nbabàm na ebem ewusiri ike;

I bu Chinekem, Onye m'nātukwasi obi.

3 N'ihi na Ya onye-ya ganaputa gi n'ibudu nke osi-ọnyà,

Na n'aka ajọ ọria nefe efe nke nëweta ila-n'iyì.

4 Nku-Ya ka O gēji kpuchie gi,

O bu kwa n'okpuru nkù-Ya abua ka i gābàba:

Ota uku na ọta di buruburu ka ezi-okwu-Ya bu.

5 I gaghi-atu egwu site n'oké egwu nke abali,

Ma-ọbu site n'àkú nke nēfeghari n'ehihie;

6 Ma-ọbu site n'ajọ ọria nefe efe nke nējeghari n'ochichiri, Ma-obu site na nbipu nke nebibi n'etiti-ehihie.

7 Nnù madu abua na ogu iri gāda n'akuku-gi; Orú nnù madu na nnù ise gäda kwa n'aka-nri-gi;

Ma o gaghi-abiaru gi nso.

8 Ọ bu nání na I gēji anya-gi abua legide,

We hu nkwughachi nke ndi nemebi iwu.

9 N'ihi na gi onwe-gi asiwo, Jehova bu ebe-nbabàm;

N'ihi na o bu Onye kachasi ihe nile elu ka i meworo ebeobibi-gi;

10 Ihe ọjọ agaghi-adakwasi gi,

Ihe-otiti agaghi-abiaru kwa nso ulo-ikwu-gi.

11 N'ihi na ndi-mo-ozi-Ya ka Ọ genye iwu bayere gi,

Idebe gi n'uzọ-gi nile.

12 N'elu obu-aka-ha ka ha gēburu gi,

Ka i ghara ikpọbì ukwu-gi na nkume.

13 Ọbuná odum na aju-ala ka i gāzọkwasi ukwu:

I gāzọbu nwa-ọdum na ogologo anu-miri.

14 N'ihi na ọ huwom n'anya si-ike, M'gēme kwa ka ọ baputa:

M'gēme ka ọ nọ n'ebe di elu, n'ihi na ọ mawo aham.

15 Ọ gākpọkum, M'gāza kwa ya;

Mu onwem gānọyere ya n'ahuhu:

M'gādọputa ya, sopuru kwa ya.

16 Ubochi ndu di ogologo ka M'gēji me ka afọ ju ya,

M'gēme kwa ka o lekwasi nzọputam anya.

91 Eni tí ó gbé ibi ìkòkọ̀ Ogá-ògo

ni yóò sinmi ní ibi òjìji Olódùmarè.

2 Èmi yóò so nípa ti OLUWA pé,

"Òun ni ààbò àti odi mi,

Olorun mi, ẹni tí èmi gbékèlé".

3 Nítòótó òun yóò gbà mí nínú

ìdèkun àwọn pẹyẹpeye

àti nínú àjàkálẹ̀-ààrùn búburú.

4 Oun yóò fi ìyé rẹ̀ bò mí,

àti ni abẹ́ ìyẹ rẹ̀ ni èmi yóò ti rí ààbò;

òtító rẹ̀ ni yóò ṣe ààbò àti odi mi.

5 Ìwọ kì yóò bẹ̀rù nítorí ẹ̀rù òru,

tàbí fún ọfà tí ń fò ní ọ̀sán,

6 Tàbí fún àjàkálẹ̀-ààrùn tí ǹ rìn kiri ní òkùnkùn,

tàbí fún ìparun tí n rìn kiri ní ọ̀sán gangan.

7 Egberún yóò subú ní ẹgbe rẹ,

ẹgbàárùn-ún ní ọwọ́ otún re

ṣùgbon kì yóò súnmó ọdọ̀ ẹ

8 Ìwo yóò máa wò ó pèlú ojú rẹ

àti wo ìjìyà àwọn ẹni búburú.

9 Nítorí ìwo fi OLUWA ṣe ààbò rẹ,

ìwo fi Ogá-ògo ṣe ibùgbé rẹ.

10 Búburú kan ki yóò subú lù ó

Bée ni ààrùnkárùn kì yóò sún mọ́ ilé rẹ.

11 Nítorí yóò fi àṣẹ fún àwọn angeli nípa tìre

láti pa ó mọ́ ní gbogbo onà re;

12   Wọn yóò gbé o sókè ní ọwọ́ wọn,

      nítorí kí ìwo má ba à fi ẹsẹ̀ rẹ gún òkúta.

13   Ìwo yóò rìn lórí kìnnìùn àti paramole;

      ìwọ yóò tẹ kìnnìún ńlá àti ejò ńlá ni ìwo yóò fi esè tè molè.

14   "Nítorí ti ìfé rẹ sí mi, èmi yóò gbà ọ́;

      èmi yóò pa o mọ́, nítorí ìwo jẹ́wọ́ orúkọ mi.

15   Òun yóò pè mí, èmi yóò sì dá a lóhùn;

      èmi yóò wà pèlú rẹ̀ nínú ìponjú,

      èmi yóò gbà á, èmi yóò sì bu ọlá fún un

16   Pèlú ẹ̀mí gígùn ni èmi yóò fi té ẹ lórùn

      èmi yóò sì fi ìgbàlà mi hàn án."

Zama a Inuwar Mai Iko Dukka

91

1 Duk wanda ya je wurin Madaukaki Zai zauna lafiya, Duk wanda yake zaune a inuwar Mai Iko Dukka,

2 Ya iya ce wa Ubangiji, "Kai ne kāriyata, da mai kiyaye ni! Kai ne Allahna, a gare ka nake dogara!"

3 Hakika zai kiyaye ka Daga dukan hatsarorin da ka ɓoye, Daga kuma dukan mugayen cuce-cuce.

4 Zai rufe ka da fikafikansa, Za ka zauna lafiya a karkashinsu. Amincinsa zai tsare ka, ya kiyaye ka.

5 Ba za ka ji tsoron hatsarori da dare ba, Ko fàdawar da za a yi maka da rana,

6 Ko annobar da take aukowa da dare, Ko mugayen da suke kisa da tsakar rana.

7 Mutum dubu za su fàɗi daura da kai, Dubu goma kuma za su fàɗi dama da kai, Amma kai, ba za a cuce ka ba.

8 Da idonka za ka duba, Ka ga yadda ake hukunta wa mugaye.

9 Domin ka dauka Ubangiji yake kiyaye ka, Madaukaki ne yake tsaronka,

10 To, ba bala'in da zai same ka, Ba za a yi wa gidanka aikin karfi da yaji ba.

11 Allah zai sa mala'ikunsa su lura da kai, Za su kiyaye ka duk inda za ka tafi.

12 Za su dauke ka a hannuwansu, Don kada ka buga kafarka a dutse.

13 Za ka tattake zakoki da macizai, Za ka tattake zakoki masu zafin rai Da macizai masu dafi.

14 Allah ya ce, "Zan ceci waɗanda suke kaunata, Zan kiyaye waɗanda suka san ni.

15 Sa'ad da suka kira gare ni, zan amsa musu, Zan kasance tare da su sa'ad da suke shan wahala, Zan cece su in girmama su.

16 Zan ba su tsawon rai lada, Hakika kuwa zan cece su."

91 Псалом. Песнь на празднование субботы.

Псалтирь 91 New Russian Translation

2   Хорошо славить Господа

    и воспевать имя Твое, Всевышний,

4   играть на десятиструнной лире

    и на мелодичной арфе.

5   Ведь Ты, Господи, обрадовал меня Своими деяниями;

    я ликую о делах Твоих рук.

6   Господи, как велики Твои дела, и как глубок

    и Твои помышления!

7   Глупый человек не знает,

    и невежда не понимает их.

8   Хотя нечестивые возникают, как трава,

    и злодеи процветают,

    они исчезнут навеки.

9   Ты же, Господи, навеки превознесен!

10 Подлинно враги Твои, Господи,

    подлинно враги Твои погибнут;

    все злодеи будут рассеяны.

11 А мой рог[a] Ты вознесешь, подобно рогу быка,

    и умастишь меня свежим маслом.

12 Глаза мои видели поражение врагов моих,

    и уши мои слышали падение злодеев, восстающих на меня.

13 А праведник цветет, словно пальма,

    возвышается, как кедр на Ливане.

14   Посаженные в доме Господнем,

        они зацветут во дворах храма нашего Бога.

15   Они и в старости будут плодовиты,сочны

        и свежи,чтобы возвещать,

16   что праведен Господь, скала моя,

        и нет в Нем неправды.

Footnotes

a. 91:11 Рог - олицетворение могущества, власти и силы.

91ישב בסתר עליון בצל שדי יתלונן.

2אמר לה' מחסי ומצודתי אלהי אבטח בו.

3כי הוא יצילך מפח יקוש מדבר הוות.

4באברתו יסך לך ותחת כנפיו תחסה צנה וסחרה אמתו.

5לא תירא מפחד לילה מחץ יעוף יומם.

6מדבר באפל יהלך מקטב ישוד צהרים.

7יפל מצדך אלף ורבבה מימינך אליך לא יגש.

8רק בעיניך תביט ושלומת רשעים תראה.

9כי אתה ה' מחסי עליון שמת מעונך.

10לא תאנה אליך רעה ונגע לא יקרב באהלך.

11כי מלאכיו יצוה לך לשמרך בכל דרכיך.

12על כפים ישאונך פן תגף באבן רגלך.

13על שחל ופתן תדרך תרמס כפיר ותנין.

14כי בי חשק ואפלטהו אשגבהו כי ידע שמי.

15יקראני ואענהו עמו אנכי בצרה אחלצהו ואכבדהו.

16ארך ימים אשביעהו ואראהו בישועתי.

91 மிக உன்னதமான ததவனிடம் மறைந்Fககாள்ள நீத
ாகமுடியும்.

சர்வ வல்லறமயுள்ள ததவனிடம்
ாFகா ்பிைைக்காகநீத ாக முடியும்.

2 நான் கர்த்தறர தநாக்கி, "நீ தர என்

ாFகா ்பிடம், என் தகாட்றட, என் ததவதன,

நான் உம்றம நம்புகிறைதன்" என்று

கூறுகிறைதன்.

3 மறைவான ஆ த்Fக்களிலிருந்Fம்

ஆத்தான தநாய்களிலிருந்Fம் ததவன் உன்றனக்
கா ாைை்றுகிைார்.

4 நீ ததவறன ாFகா ்பிைைக்காக அணுகமுடியும்.

அவர் உன்றன ஒரு றைவ சிறைக

விரித்Fத் தன் குஞ்சுகறளக் கா றத ்த ான்று

கா ார்.

ததவன் ஒரு தகடகத்றத ்த ான்றைமும்
சுவறர ்த ாண ்மும் உன்றன ்
ாFகாக்கிைார்.

5 இரவில் நீ அஞ்சத்தக்கFஎFவுமில்றல.

நீ கலில் றகவரின் அம்புக்கும் ய ்டமாட்டாய்.

6 இருளில் வரும் ககாடிய தநாய்களுக்கும்,

நடு கலில் வரும் ககாடிய தநாய்களுக்கும் நீ அஞ்
சமாட்டாய்.

7 நீ ஆயிரம் றகவர்கறளத் ததாறைை்கடி ாய்.

உன் கசாந்த வலFக தினாயிரம்
றகவீரர்கறளத் ததாறைை்கடிக்கும்.

உன் றகவர்கள் உன்றனத்
ததாடக்கூடமாட்டார்கள்.

8 சை்று ார்,

அத்தீதயார் தண்டிக்க ்ட்டறத நீ காண ாய்!

9 ஏகனனில் நீ கர்த்தறர நம்புகிைாய்.

மிக உன்னதமான ததவறன நீ உன்

ொாΓகா ஂபிடமாகக்ககாண்டாய்.

10 தீயறவ உனக்கு நிகழாΓ,

உன் வீட்டில் எந்தவிதமான தநாய்களும் இரு ஂதில்
றல.

11 ததவன் அவரΓதூதர்கறள உனக்காகக்
கட்டறளயிடுவார்.

நீத ொகுமிடங்களிகலல்லாம் அவர்கள் உன்றன ஂ
ொாΓகா ஂொர்கள்.

12 உன் கால் ொறறயில் தமாதாத டிக்கு

அவர்கள் றகஂகள் உன்றன ஂபிடித்Fக்ககாள்ளும்

13 சிங்கங்களின் தமலும்

விஷம் நிரம்பிய ொாம்புகளின் தமலும் நடக்கும்

வல்லறம உனக்கு வாய்க்கும்.

14 கர்த்தர்: "ஒருவன் என்றன நம்பினால், நான்
அவறன மீத்தன்.

என் நாமத்றத கதாழுΓக்ககாண்டு என்றன ஂபின்
ஂஂற்றுதவாறரநான் க ஂொறஂற்றுதவன்" என்
கிறொஂொர்.

15 என்றன ஂபின் ஂற்றுதவார் உதவிக்காக என்றன
அறழ ஂொர்கள்.

நான் அவர்களுக்கு ஂதில் ககாடு ஂதன்.

அவர்களுக்குத் கதால்றல தநரும்த ொாΓ நான்
அவர்கதளாடு இரு ஂத ன்.

நான் அவர்கறளக் கா ஂொறஂறி ஂக ஂறம ஂ
டுத்Fதவன்.

16 என்றன ஂபின் ஂற்றுதவாருக்கு நான் நீண்ட ஆ புறளாக்
ககாடு ஂத ன்.

நான் அவர்கறளக் கா ஂொறஂஂற்றுதவன்.

1 तुम परम परमेश्वर की शरण में िहपने के िहये जा सकते ि◌ो।

 तुम सर्वशक्तिमान परमेश्वर की शरण में संरक्षण पाने को जा सकते ि◌ो।

2 मैं यीर्◌ा से हर्नती करता हूँ, "तू मेरा सुरक्षा स्थि ि◌ मेरा गढ़,

 ि◌ परमेश्वर, मैं तेरे भरोसे हूँ।"

3 परमेश्वर तुझको सभी िहपे खतरों से बचाएगा। परमेश्वर

 तुझको सब भयानक व्याहियों से बचाएगा।

4 तुम परमेश्वर की शरण में संरक्षण पाने को जा सकते ि◌ो।

 और र्◌ि तुम्हारी ऐसे रक्षा करेगा जैसे एक पक्षी अपने पंख फै ि◌ा कर अपने

बच्◌ों की रक्षा करता ि◌ ।

5 रात में तुमको हकसी का भय निी ि◌ोगा,

 और शत्रु के बाणों से तू हिन में भयभीत निी ि◌ोगा।

6 तुझको अंि◌रे में आने र्◌ाि◌ रोगों

 और उस भयानक रोग से जो ि◌ोपिर में आता ि◌ भय निी ि◌ोगा।

7 तू ि◌जार शत्रुओं को पराहजत कर ि◌गा।

 तेरा स्वयं ि◌ाहिना ि◌ाथ ि◌स ि◌जार शत्रुओं को ि◌रायेगा

 । और तेरे शत्रु तुझको ि◌ ꠷ तक निीपायेंगे।

8 जरा ि◌ेख, और तुझको हिखाई ि◌गा

 हक र्◌े कु हि◌ व्यक्ति ि◌क्तित ि◌ो चुके ि◌ें।

9 क्◌ो ST ि◌ क्◌ोहक तू यीर्◌ा के भरोसे ि◌ ।

 तूने परम परमेश्वर को अपना शरणस्थि बनाया ि◌ ।

10 तेरे साथ कोई भी बुरी बात निी घिगी।

 कोई भी रोग तेरे घर में निी ि◌ोगा।

11 क्◌ोहक परमेश्वर स्वगर्वूितों को तेरी रक्षा करने का आि◌श ि◌गा। तू जि◌ाँ ꠷ भी जाएगा र्◌े तेरी

 रक्षा करेंगे।

12 परमेश्वर के ि◌꠷ त तुझको अपने ि◌ाथों पर ऊपर

 उठायेंगे। ताहक तेरा पैर चट्टान से न ि◌कराए।

13 तुझमें र्◌ि शक्ति ि◌ोगी हजससे तू हसि◌ों को

पिडेगा और हर्ष नागों को कु चि ि़ंगा।

14 यिोर्ा किता ि़ै, "यहि कोई जन मुझ में भरोसा रखता ि़ै तो मैं उसकी रक्षा करूँ गा। मैं उन भिों को जो मेरे नाम की आराि़ना करते ि़ं, संरक्षप ि़ूँगा।"

15 मेरे भि मुझको ि़ोरा पाने को पुकरेंगे और मैं उनकी सुनूँगा।
र॒े जब कष्ट में ि़ोग मैं उनके साथ रहूँगा।
मैं उनका उद्धार करूँ गा और उन्हें आिर ि़ूँगा।

16 मैं अपने अनुयाहप्यों को एक ि़म्बी आयु
ि़ूँगा और मैं उनकीरक्षा करूँ गा।

91جوشخص اللہ تعالیٰ کے پناہ میں رہتا ہے خدا کے سائے میں جا کتے ہو.

تو حفاظت کے لئے خدا قادرِ مطلق کے پناہ میں جا سکتے ہو.

خداوند سے کہتا ہوں، تو میری پناہ اور میرا قلعہ ہے.

خدا، میں تجھ پر توکل رکھتا ہوں. تُو تیرے

فنجات کو جھوٹ پوشیدہ خطروں سے بچائے گا.

خدا تجھے کو تباہ کرنے والی کبھی مہاماریوں سے بچائے گا.

وہ خدا کے پناہ میں جاؤ و میری حفاظت کے لئے بچا کتے ہو. اور وہ تمہاری ساری

حفاظت کر کے گا جیسے پرندہ اپنے پر پر بھی الکر اپنے بچوں

کی حفاظت کرتا ہے.

خدا تمہاری حفاظت سپر اور محفوظ دیواری کی طرح کرے گا.

تو رات میں تو کسی کا خوف نہ ہوگا.

اور دن کے تیروں سے دن میں خطرہ نہ ہی ہوگا.

اور تو شریروں کی ہزار نقصانوں کو گرا دے گا.

اور تیرے دس منٹ تجھ کو چھوت کنہیں پہنچائیں گے.

اگر آنکھ اٹھ تو دیکھ لے کہ کس طرح ظالم ملک ہو رہے ہیں.

کیوں؟ اس لئے کہ تو نے خداوند کو بلند ترین پناہ بنا لیا ہے.

تو نے خدا قادرِ مطلق کو اپنی پناہ بنا لیا ہے.

اس لئے تجھ کو کوئی بُرائی پر چھو بات نہیں ہوگی.

اور کوئی وبا بیماری حی تیری جھمک کے نزدیک نہ پہنچ سکے گی.

کیوں کہ خدا فرشتوں کو تیری حفاظت کرنے کا حکم دے گا.

تو جہاں بھی جا ئوگے وہ تیری حفاظت کریں گے یہ فرشتے تجھے اپنے

ہاتھوں پر اٹھا لیں گے تاکہ

تاکہ میرا پاؤں بھی پتھر سے نہ ٹکرائے.

اور شیر اور ناگ کو روند ڈالے گا.

سنگ سے تیش لائی بوں کو پی چھا ڈال دے گا۔ زمین کے

رنگوں کو کک چل دے گا اور

4 خداوند کہتا ہے، 'کہ کوئی شخص مجھ میں بھروسہ رکھتا ہے تو میں اس کی

حفاظت کروں گا.

میں ان لوگوں کی جو میرے نام کی عبادت کرتے ہیں، حفاظت کروں گا اور لوگ مجھ کو پکاری رہیں گے

تو میں ان کے ساتھ ہی رہوں گا لمیں ملیں

چھڑاؤں گ

او ع زندہ کروں گا.

16میں اپنے سے پھر کار کو تک طول زندگی

دوں گا، میں ان کی حفاظت کروں گا." اور

91 ئەوەی لە پەناگای هەرەبەرز دادەنیشت

ئەوەی لە سێبەری خودای هەرە بە توانا دەمێنێتەوە،

2 بە یەزدان دەڵێ: «تۆ پەناگامی، قەڵامی،
خودای من، پشتت پێ دەبەستم.»

3 چونکە لە تۆڕی ڕاوچی دەربازت دەکات،
لە دەرد و بەڵای کوشندە،

4 بە باڵی خۆی داتدەپۆشێت،
لەژێر باڵەکانی پەنا دەگریت، و
دڵسۆزییەکەی قەڵغان و سوورایە.

5 نە لە ترۆقینی شەو دەترسیت، و
نە لەو تیرەی بە ڕۆژ دەهاوێژرێت،

6 نە لەو دەردەی کە لە تاریکی دێت،
نە لەو ئافاتەی بە ڕۆژی نیوەڕۆ زیان دەبەخشێت.

7 هەزار کەس لە تەنیشتت بەردەبنەوە،
دە هەزار لەلای دەستە ڕاستت،
بەڵام لە تۆ نزیک ناکەوێتەوە.

8 بەڵکو تەنها بە چاوی خۆت سەیر دەکەیت، و
سزای بەدکاران دەبینیت.

9 چونکە یەزدانت کرد بە پەناگات،
هەرەبەرزت کرد بە لانەی خۆت،

10 هیچ خراپەیەکت بەسەرنایەت، و
هیچ بەڵایەک لە ماڵت نزیک ناکەوێتەوە.

11 لەبەر ئەوەی سەبارەت بە تۆ فەرمان بە فریشتەکانی دەدات،
بۆ ئەوەی لە هەموو هەنگاوێکت بپارێزن،

12 لەسەر دەستیان هەڵتدەگرن،
تاکو پێت بەر بەردێک نەکەوێت.

13 پێ بە شێر و ماری کۆبرادا دەنێیت،
بەجگە شێر و ئەژدیها پێشێل دەکەیت.

14 یەزدان دەفەرموێت: «لەبەر ئەوەی دڵی بە منەوە بەندە، ڕزگاری دەکەم،
دەیپارێزم، چونکە من دەناسێت[a].

15 نزام بۆ دەکات، وەڵامی دەدەمەوە،
لە تەنگانەدا لەگەڵیدام،
دەربازی دەکەم و ڕێزداری دەکەم.

16 بە ڕۆژگاری درێژ تێری دەکەم،
ڕزگاریی خۆمی نیشان دەدەم.»

Footnotes

a. 14:91 بە واتای ناسینی خودا و کەسایەتییەکەی.

91 الساكِنُ تَحتَ سِترِ العَليِّ،
تُظَلِّلُهُ حِمايَةُ القَديرِ.
[2] أقُولُ للهِ الَّذِي أتَّكِلُ عَلَيهِ:
«أنتَ إلَهِي وَمَلجَأيَ وَحِصنِي!»
[3] مِنَ الفَخِّ سَيُنقِذُكَ
سَيُنقِذُكَ مِنَ المُصِيبَةِ وَالأوبِئَةِ.
[4] سَيَفرِدُ جَناحَيهِ فَوقَكَ.
وَيَدعُكَ تَحتَمِي تَحتَ جَناحَيهِ.
وَسَيَكُونُ إخلاصُهُ سِياجًا حامِيًا حَولَكَ!
[5] لَن تَخشَى مِنْ رُعبِ اللَّيلِ،
وَلا مِنْ سِهامِ العَدُوِّ الطّائِرَةِ فِي النَّهارِ!
[6] لَن تَخشَى مِنْ مَرَضٍ يَنتَشِرُ فِي الخَفاءِ.
وَلا مِنْ وَباءٍ يَضرِبُ عِندَ الظُّهرِ.
[7] ألفٌ مِنْ جُنُودِ الأعادِي سَيَتساقَطُونَ حَولَكَ.
وَعَشَرَةُ الآفِ سَيَتساقَطُونَ بِسَمْبِكَ،
لَن يُؤذِيَكَ أيٌّ مِنهُمْ!
[8] أجَلْ، بِأُمِّ عَينَيكَ سَتَرَى كُلَّ هَذا!
سَتَرَى الأشرارَ يَنالُونَ ما يَستَحِقُّونَ!
[9] لِأنَّكَ جَعَلتَ اللهَ مَلجَأكَ،
وَالعَليَّ مَسكِنَكَ الآمِنَ.
[10] لِهَذا ما مِنْ مُصِيبَةٍ سَتُصِيبُكَ.
وَما مِنْ وَباءٍ سَيَدخُلُ مَسكِنَكَ.
[11] لِأنَّهُ يُوصِي مَلائِكَتَهُ بِكَ
لِكَي يَحرُسُوكَ حَيثُما تَذهَبُ!
[12] سَيَحمِلُونَكَ عَلَى أيادِيهِمْ،
لِئَلّا تَرتَطِمَ قَدَمُكَ بِحَجَرٍ.
[13] عَلَى الأسَدِ وَالأفعَى تَدُوسُ،
وَتَطَأُ الشِّبلَ وَالثُّعبانَ!
[14] فَكَما يَقُولُ اللهُ:
«يُحِبُّنِي، لِهَذا سَأُنقِذُهُ!
سَأُرَفِّعُهُ لِأنَّهُ يَعرِفُ اسْمِي.
[15] يَستَنجِدُ بِي فَأستَجِيبُ.
فِي وَقتِ الضِّيقِ أكُونُ مَعَهُ.
أُنقِذُهُ وَأُكَرِّمُهُ.
[16] أُعطِيهِ عُمرًا طَوِيلًا،
وَأُرِيهِ خَلاصِي.»

Psalm 91 - God Is Our Protector

1 He who dwells in the shelter of the Most High

   will rest in the shadow of the Almighty.[a]

2 I will say [b] of the LORD, "He is my refuge and my fortress,

   my God, in whom I trust."

3 Surely he will save you from the fowler's snare

   and from the deadly pestilence.

4 He will cover you with his feathers,

   and under his wings you will find refuge;

   his faithfulness will be your shield and rampart.

5 You will not fear the terror of night,

   nor the arrow that flies by day,

6 nor the pestilence that stalks in the darkness,

   nor the plague that destroys at midday.

7 A thousand may fall at your side,

   ten thousand at your right hand,

   but it will not come near you.

8 You will only observe with your eyes

   and see the punishment of the wicked.

9 If you make the Most High your dwelling.

   even the LORD, who is my refuge-

10 then no harm will befall you,

   no disaster will come near your tent.

11 For he will command his angels concerning you

   to guard you in all your ways;

12 they will lift you up in their hands,

   so that you will not strike your foot against a stone.

Psalm 91 Evangelical Heritage Version

Psalm 91

The Shadow of Your Wings

The General Principle

1   One who lives in the shelter of the Most High
    will stay in the shadow of the Almighty.

Application to Oneself

2   I will say to the LORD,
    "My refuge and my fortress, my God in whom I trust."

Application to Others

3   Surely he will rescue you from the fowler's trap,
    from the destructive plague.

4   With his feathers he will cover you,
    and under his wings you will find refuge.
    His truth will be your shield and armor.

5   You will not fear the terror of night,
    nor the arrow that flies by day,

6   nor the plague that prowls in the darkness,
    nor the pestilence that destroys at noon.

7   A thousand may fall at your side,
    ten thousand at your right hand,
    but it will not come near you.

8   You will only observe it with your eyes,
    You will see the punishment of the wicked.

Application to Oneself

9   Yes, you, LORD, are my refuge!
    If you make the Most High your shelter,

Application to Others

10   evil will not overtake you.
    Disaster will not come near your tent.
11   Yes, he will give a command to his angels concerning you,
    to guard you in all your ways.
12   They will lift you up in their hands,
    so that you will not strike your foot against a stone.
13   You will tread on the lion and the cobra.
    You will trample the young lion and the serpent.

God;s Promise of Delivery

14   The LORD says,[a]
    Because he clings to me, I will rescue him.
    I will protect him, because he acknowledges my name.
15   He will call on me, and I will answer him.
    I will be with him in distress.
    I will deliver him and I will honor him.
16   With long life I will satisfy him,
    and I will let him see my salvation.

Footnotes

a. Psalm 91:14 The words the LORD says are added to make it clear who is speaking.

Psalm 91 English Standard Version

My Refuge and My Fortress

91 He who dwells in the shelter of the Most High

    will abide in the shadow of the Almighty.

2   I will say[a] to the LORD, "My refuge and my fortress,

    my God, in whom I trust."

3   For he will deliver you from the snare of the fowler

    and from the deadly pestilence.

4   He will cover you with his pinions,

    and under his wings you will find refuge;

    his faithfulness is a shield and buckler.

5   You will not fear the terror of the night,

    nor the arrow that flies by day,

6   nor the pestilence that stalks in darkness,

    nor the destruction that wastes at noonday.

7   A thousand may fall at your side,

    ten thousand at your right hand,

    but it will not come near you.

8   You will only look with your eyes

    and see the recompense of the wicked.

9   Because you have made the LORD your dwelling place—

    the Most High, who is my refuge[b]

10   no evil shall be allowed to befall you,

    no plague come near your tent.

11   For he will command his angels concerning you

    to guard you in all your ways.

12   On their hands they will bear you up,

      lest you strike your foot against a stone.

13   You will tread on the lion and the adder;

      the young lion and the serpent you will trample underfoot.

14   "Because he holds fast to me in love, I will deliver him;

      I will protect him, because he knows my name.

15   When he calls to me, I will answer him;

      I will be with him in trouble;

      I will rescue him and honor him.

16   With long life I will satisfy him

      and show him my salvation."

Footnotes

a. Psalm 91:2 Septuagint He will say

b. Psalm 91:9 Or For you, O LORD, are my refuge! You have made the Most High your dwelling place

Psalm 91 Good News Translation

God Our Protector

91 Whoever goes to the LORD for safety,

whoever remains under the protection of the Almighty,

2 can say to him,

"You are my defender and protector.

You are my God; in you I trust."

3 He will keep you safe from all hidden dangers

and from all deadly diseases.

4 He will cover you with his wings;

you will be safe in his care;

his faithfulness will protect and defend you.

5 You need not fear any dangers at night

or sudden attacks during the day

6 or the plagues that strike in the dark

or the evils that kill in daylight.

7 A thousand may fall dead beside you,

ten thousand all around you,

but you will not be harmed.

8 You will look and see

how the wicked are punished.

9 You have made the LORD your[a] defender,

the Most High your protector,

10 and so no disaster will strike you,

no violence will come near your home.

11 God will put his angels in charge of you

to protect you wherever you go.

12   They will hold you up with their hands

to keep you from hurting your feet on the stones.

13   You will trample down lions and snakes,

fierce lions and poisonous snakes.

14   God says, "I will save those who love me

and will protect those who acknowledge me as LORD.

15   When they call to me, I will answer them;

when they are in trouble, I will be with them.

I will rescue them and honor them.

16   I will reward them with long life;

I will save them."

Footnotes

a. <u>Psalm 91:9</u> Probable text your; Hebrew my.

Psalm 91 Douay-Rheims 1899 American Edition

91 A psalm of a canticle on the sabbath day.

2 It is good to give praise to the Lord: and to sing to thy name, O most High.

3 To shew forth thy mercy in the morning, and thy truth in the night:

4 Upon an instrument of ten strings, upon the psaltery: with a canticle upon the harp.

5 For thou hast given me, O Lord, a delight in thy doings: and in the works of thy hands I shall rejoice.

6 O Lord, how great are thy works! thy thoughts are exceeding deep.

7 The senseless man shall not know: nor will the fool understand these things.

8 When the wicked shall spring up as grass: and all the workers of iniquity shall appear: That they may perish for ever and ever:

9 But thou, O Lord, art most high for evermore.

10 For behold thy enemies, O Lord, for behold thy enemies shall perish: and all the workers of iniquity shall be scattered.

11 But my horn shall be exalted like that of the unicorn: and my old age in plentiful mercy.

12 My eye also hath looked down upon my enemies: and my ear shall hear of the downfall of the malignant that rise up against me.

13 The just shall flourish like the palm tree: he shall grow up like the cedar of Libanus.

14 They that are planted in the house of the Lord shall flourish in the courts of the house of our God.

15 They shall still increase in a fruitful old age: and shall be well treated,

16 That they may shew, That the Lord our God is righteous, and there is no iniquity in him.

Psalm 91 New American Bible (Revised Edition)

Psalm 91[a]

Security Under God's Protection

I

1 You who dwell in the shelter of the Most High,[b]
    who abide in the shade of the Almighty,

2 Say to the LORD, "My refuge and fortress,
    my God in whom I trust."

3 He will rescue you from the fowler's snare,
    from the destroying plague,

4 He will shelter you with his pinions,
    and under his wings you may take refuge;
    his faithfulness is a protecting shield.

5 You shall not fear the terror of the night
    nor the arrow that flies by day,

6 Nor the pestilence that roams in darkness,
    nor the plague that ravages at noon.

7 Though a thousand fall at your side,
    ten thousand at your right hand,
    near you it shall not come.

8 You need simply watch;
    the punishment of the wicked you will see.

9 Because you have the LORD for your refuge
    and have made the Most High your stronghold,

10 No evil shall befall you,
    no affliction come near your tent.

11   [c] For he commands his angels with regard to you,
        to guard you wherever you go.

12   With their hands they shall support you,
        lest you strike your foot against a stone.

13   You can tread upon the asp and the viper,
        trample the lion and the dragon.

II

14   Because he clings to me I will deliver him;
        because he knows my name I will set him on high.

15   He will call upon me and I will answer;
        I will be with him in distress;
        I will deliver him and give him honor.

16   With length of days I will satisfy him,
        and fill him with my saving power.

Footnotes

a. Psalm 91 A prayer of someone who has taken refuge in the Lord, possibly within the Temple (Ps 91:1–2). The psalmist is confident that God's presence will protect the people in every dangerous situation (Ps 91:3-13). The final verses are an oracle of salvation promising salvation to those who trust in God (Ps 91:14-16).

b. 91:1 **The shelter of the Most High**: basically "hiding place" but in the Psalms a designation for the protected Temple precincts, cf. Ps 27:5; 31:21; 61:5. **The shade of the Almighty**: lit., "the shadow of the wings of the Almighty," cf. Ps 17:8; 36:8; 57:2; 63:8. Ps 91:4 makes clear that the shadow is an image of the safety afforded by the outstretched wings of the cherubim in the holy of holies.

c. 91:11-12 The words are cited in Lk 4:10–11; Mt 4:6, as Satan tempts Jesus in the desert.

The Lord-the One We Trust

91 He who lives in the safe place of the Most High will be in the shadow of the All-powerful. **2** I will say to the Lord, "You are my safe and strong place, my God, in Whom I trust." **3** For it is He Who takes you away from the trap, and from the killing sickness. **4** He will cover you with His wings. And under His wings you will be safe. He is faithful like a safe-covering and a strong wall.

5 You will not be afraid of trouble at night, or of the arrow that flies by day. **6** You will not be afraid of the sickness that walks in darkness, or of the trouble that destroys at noon. **7** A thousand may fall at your side, and ten thousand at your right hand. But it will not come near you. **8** You will only look on with your eyes, and see how the sinful are punished. **9** Because you have made the Lord your safe place, and the Most High the place where you live, **10** nothing will hurt you. No trouble will come near your tent.

11 For He will tell His angels to care for you and keep you in all your ways. **12** They will hold you up in their hands. So your foot will not hit against a stone. **13** You will walk upon the lion and the snake. You will crush under your feet the young lion and the snake.

14 Because he has loved Me, I will bring him out of trouble. I will set him in a safe place on high, because he has known My name. **15** He will call upon Me, and I will answer him. I will be with him in trouble. I will take him out of trouble and honor him. **16** I will please him with a long life. And I will show him My saving power.

Psalm 91 New Revised Standard Version, Anglicised Catholic Edition

Psalm 91

Assurance of God's Protection

1   You who live in the shelter of the Most High,
      who abide in the shadow of the Almighty,[a]

2   will say to the LORD, 'My refuge and my fortress;
      my God, in whom I trust.

3   For he will deliver you from the snare of the fowler

4   and from the deadly pestilence;

5   he will cover you with his pinions,
      and under his wings you will find refuge;
      his faithfulness is a shield and buckler.

6   You will not fear the terror of the night,
      or the arrow that flies by day,

7   or the pestilence that stalks in darkness,
      or the destruction that wastes at noonday.

8   A thousand may fall at your side,
      ten thousand at your right hand,
      but it will not come near you.

9   You will only look with your eyes
      and see the punishment of the wicked.

10   Because you have made the LORD your refuge,[b]
      the Most High your dwelling-place,
      no evil shall befall you,
      no scourge come near your tent.

11.   For he will command his angels concerning you to
      guard you in all your ways.

12   On their hands they will bear you up,
      so that you will not dash your foot against a stone.

13   You will tread on the lion and the adder,
      the young lion and the serpent you will trample under foot.

14   Those who love me, I will deliver;
      I will protect those who know my name.

15   When they call to me, I will answer them;
      I will be with them in trouble,

16   With long life I will satisfy them,
      and show them my salvation.

Footnotes

a. Psalm 91:1 Traditional rendering of Heb *Shaddai*
b. Psalm 91:9 Cn: Heb *Because you, LORD, are my refuge; you have made*

Psalm 91 New Revised Standard Version Catholic Edition

Psalm 91

Assurance of God's Protection

1   You who live in the shelter of the Most High,
       who abide in the shadow of the Almighty, [a]

2   will say to the LORD, "My refuge and my fortress;
       my God, in whom I trust."

3   For he will deliver you from the snare of the fowler
       and from the deadly pestilence;

4   he will cover you with his pinions,
       and under his wings you will find refuge;
       his faithfulness is a shield and buckler.

5   You will not fear the terror of the night,
       or the arrow that flies by day,

6   or the pestilence that stalks in darkness,
       or the destruction that wastes at noonday.

7   A thousand may fall at your side,
       ten thousand at your right hand,
       but it will not come near you.

8   You will only look with your eyes

    and see the punishment of the wicked.

9   Because you have made the LORD your refuge, [b]

    the Most High your dwelling place,

10 no evil shall befall you,

    no scourge come near your tent.

11 For he will command his angels concerning you

    to guard you in all your ways.

12 On their hands they will bear you up,

    so that you will not dash your foot against a stone.

13 You will tread on the lion and the adder,

    the young lion and the serpent you will trample under foot.

14 Those who love me, I will deliver;

    I will protect those who know my name.

15 When they call to me, I will answer them;

    I will be with them in trouble,

    I will rescue them and honor them.

16 With long life I will satisfy them,

    and show them my salvation.

Footnotes

a. Psalm 91:1 Traditional rendering of Heb *Shaddai*

b. Psalm 91:9 Cn: Heb *Because you, LORD, are my refuge; you have made*

Psalm 91   New Revised Standard Version, Anglicised

Psalm 91

Assurance of God's Protection

1   You who live in the shelter of the Most High,
      who abide in the shadow of the Almighty,[a]

2   will say to the LORD, 'My refuge and my fortress;
      my God, in whom I trust.

3   For he will deliver you from the snare of the fowler
      and from the deadly pestilence;

4   he will cover you with his pinions,
      and under his wings you will find refuge;
      his faithfulness is a shield and buckler.

5   You will not fear the terror of the night,
      or the arrow that flies by day,

6   or the pestilence that stalks in darkness,
      or the destruction that wastes at noonday.

7   A thousand may fall at your side,
      ten thousand at your right hand,
      but it will not come near you.

8   You will only look with your eyes
      and see the punishment of the wicked.

9   Because you have made the LORD your refuge,[b]
      the Most High your dwelling-place,

Daisy Ngozichukwuka Obi | 9C

10   no evil shall befall you,
          no scourge come near your tent.

11   For he will command his angels concerning you
          to guard you in all your ways.

12   On their hands they will bear you up,
          so that you will not dash your foot against a stone.

13   You will tread on the lion and the adder,
          the young lion and the serpent you will trample under foot.

14   Those who love me, I will deliver;
          I will protect those who know my name.

15   When they call to me, I will answer them;
          I will be with them in trouble,
          I will rescue them and honour them.

16   With long life I will satisfy them,
          and show them my salvation

Footnotes.

a. Psalm 91:1 Traditional rendering of Heb Shaddai

b. Psalm 91:9 Cn: Heb Because you, LORD, are my refuge; you have made

Psalm 91 Amplified Bible, Classic Edition

Psalm 91

[1] He who [a]dwells in the secret place of the Most High shall remain stable and fixed under the shadow of the Almighty [Whose power no foe can withstand].

[2] I will say of the Lord, He is my Refuge and my Fortress, my God; on Him I lean and rely, and in Him I [confidently] trust!

[3] For [then] He will deliver you from the snare of the fowler and from the deadly pestilence.

[4] [Then] He will cover you with His pinions, and under His wings shall you trust and find refuge; His truth and His faithfulness are a shield and a buckler.

[5] You shall not be afraid of the terror of the night, nor of the arrow (the evil plots and slanders of the wicked) that flies by day,

[6] Nor of the pestilence that stalks in darkness, nor of the destruction and sudden death that surprise and lay waste at noonday.

[7] A thousand may fall at your side, and ten thousand at your right hand, but it shall not come near you.

[8] Only a spectator shall you be [yourself inaccessible in the secret place of the Most High] as you witness the reward of the wicked.

[9] Because you have made the Lord your refuge, and the Most High your dwelling place,

[10] There shall no evil befall you, nor any plague or calamity come near your

tent.

11 For He will give His angels [especial] charge over you to accompany and defend and preserve you in all your ways [of obedience and service].

12 They shall bear you up on their hands, lest you dash your foot against a stone.

13 You shall tread upon the lion and adder; the young lion and the serpent shall you trample underfoot.

14 Because he has set his love upon Me, therefore will I deliver him; I will set him on high, because he knows and understands My name [has a personal knowledge of My mercy, love, and kindness-trusts and relies on Me, knowing I will never forsake him, no, never].

15 He shall call upon Me, and I will answer him; I will be with him in trouble, I will deliver him and honor him.

16 With long life will I satisfy him and show him My salvation.

Footnotes

a. Psalm 91:1 The rich promises of this whole chapter are dependent upon one's meeting exactly the conditions of these first two verses (see Exod. 15:26).

Psalm 91 New Catholic Bible

Psalm 91[a]

Security under God's Protection

1   You who abide in the shelter of the Most High,[b]
      who rest in the shadow of the Almighty,

2   say to the LORD, "You are my refuge and my fortress,
      my God in whom I place my trust."

3   He will rescue you from the snare of the fowler[c]
      and from virulent pestilence.

4   With his feathers he will shelter you,[d]
      and you will take refuge under his wings;
      his faithfulness serves as a protective shield.

5   You will not fear the terror by night[e]
      nor the arrow that flies by day,

6   nor the pestilence that stalks in darkness,
      nor the plague[f] that lays waste at midday.

7   Even though a thousand may fall at your side,
      ten thousand at your right hand,
      such evils will not afflict you.

8   Rather, your own eyes will behold[g]
      the punishment inflicted on the wicked.

9   You have made the LORD your refuge
      and chosen the Most High to be your dwelling.

10   Therefore, no evil will threaten you,
      no calamity will come near your dwelling.

11   [h] For he will command his angels[i] about you–
      to guard you wherever you go.

12   They will lift you up with their hands,
      lest you dash your foot against a stone.[j]

13   You will tread upon the asp and the viper;
you will trample the lion and the dragon.[k]

14 ["Because he loves me, I will deliver him,
    I will raise high[m] the one who acknowledges my name.
15 When he calls to me, I will answer,
    and I will be with him in time of distress;
    I will rescue him and cause him to be honored.[n]
16 I will reward him with a long life
    and show him my salvation."[o]

Footnotes

a. Psalm 91:1 This pilgrimage psalm is a glowing testimony to the security that God bestows on those who come to the temple to place themselves under his protection. They will be strengthened by God and his angels all along the path of life in which perils and snares proliferate on every side: the terror by night, the arrow by day, the fowler's snare, pestilence, and plague, as well as the asp and viper, lion and dragon-in a word, every possible threat. Death itself seems to retreat, and one gets a glimpse of the peace and joy of the Messianic Age.

En route toward Jerusalem, or toward God, every believer is a pilgrim. The itinerary is not an idyllic dream; rather, amidst risks and dangers, the Lord delivers us from fear and leads us to salvation, to life in his presence. This peaceful psalm is especially suited to be an evening prayer.

We can regard this psalm as an exhortation of Christ developing the invitation that he addressed to his disciples after the Last Supper: "Do not let your hearts be troubled. You place your trust in God [the Father]. Trust also in me" (Jn 14:1). We are to journey along the path of life with the constant certitude that the divine Persons surround us with a never- ending solicitude.

b. Psalm 91:1 The shelter of the Most High: a designation in the psalms for the temple (see Pss 27:5; 31:21; 61:5). The shadow of the Almighty: literally, "the shadow of the wings of the Almighty" (see Pss 17:8; 36:8;

Psalm 91 Easy-to-Read Version

91 You can go to God Most High to hide.

You can go to God All-Powerful for protection.

2 I say to the LORD, "You are my place of safety, my fortress.

My God, I trust in you."

3 God will save you from hidden dangers

and from deadly diseases.

4 You can go to him for protection.

He will cover you like a bird spreading its wings over its babies.

You can trust him to surround and protect you like a shield.

5 You will have nothing to fear at night

and no need to be afraid of enemy arrows during the day.

6 You will have no fear of diseases that come in the dark

or terrible suffering that comes at noon.

7 A thousand people may fall dead at your side

or ten thousand right beside you,

but nothing bad will happen to you!

8 All you will have to do is watch,

and you will see that the wicked are punished.

9 You trust in the LORD for protection.

You have made God Most High your place of safety.

10 So nothing bad will happen to you.

No diseases will come near your home.

11 He will command his angels to protect you wherever you go.

12 Their hands will catch you

so that you will not hit your foot on a rock.

13 You will have power to trample on lions

and poisonous snakes.

14 The Lord says, "If someone trusts me, I will save them.

I will protect my followers who call to me for help.

¹⁵ When my followers call to me, I will answer them.
I will be with them when they are in trouble.
I will rescue them and honor them.
¹⁶ I will give my followers a long life
and show them my power to save."

Psalm 91 Christian Standard Bible

Psalm 91

The Protection of the Most High

1   The one who lives under the protection of the Most High
     dwells in the shadow of the Almighty.
2   I will say[a] concerning the LORD, who is my refuge and my
     fortress, my God in whom I trust:
3   He himself will rescue you from the bird trap,
     from the destructive plague.
4   He will cover you with his feathers;
     you will take refuge under his wings.
     His faithfulness will be a protective shield.
5   You will not fear the terror of the night,
     the arrow that flies by day,
6   the plague that stalks in darkness,
     or the pestilence that ravages at noon.
7   Though a thousand fall at your side
     and ten thousand at your right hand,
     the pestilence will not reach you.
8   You will only see it with your eyes
     and witness the punishment of the wicked.
9   Because you have made the LORD-my refuge,
     the Most High-your dwelling place,
10   no harm will come to you;
     no plague will come near your tent.
11   For he will give his angels orders concerning you,
     to protect you in all your ways.
12   They will support you with their hands
     so that you will not strike your foot against a stone.
13   You will tread on the lion and the cobra;
     you will trample the young lion and the serpent.

14	Because he has his heart set on me,
	I will deliver him;
	I will protect him because he knows my name.
15	When he calls out to me, I will answer him;
	I will be with him in trouble.
	I will rescue him and give him honor.
16	I will satisfy him with a long life
	and show him my salvation.

Footnotes

a. 91:1–2 LXX, Syr, Jer read ² Almighty, saying, or ² Almighty, he will say

Psalm 91 Jubilee Bible 2000

[1] He that dwells in the secret place of the most High shall abide under the shadow of the Almighty.

[2] I will say of the LORD, He is my hope and my fortress: my God; in him will I secure myself.

[3] Surely he shall deliver thee from the snare of the fowler and from the mortal pestilence.

[4] He shall cover thee with his feathers, and under his wings thou shalt be secure: his truth shall be thy shield and buckler.

[5] Thou shalt not be afraid for the terror by night, nor for the arrow that flies by day,

[6] nor for the pestilence that walks in darkness, nor for the destruction that wastes at noonday.

[7] Thousands shall fall at thy side and ten thousands at thy right hand, but it shall not come near thee.

[8] Surely with thine eyes thou shalt behold and see the reward of the wicked.

[9] Because thou hast made the LORD, who is my hope, even the most High, thy habitation,

[10] no evil shall befall thee, neither shall any plague come near thy dwelling.

[11] For he shall give his angels charge over thee to keep thee in all thy ways.

[12] They shall bear thee up in their hands lest thy foot stumble against a stone.

¹³ Thou shalt tread upon the lion and adder; the young lion and the dragon shalt thou trample under feet.

¹⁴ Because he has set his will upon me, therefore I will deliver him; I will set him on high because he has known my name.

¹⁵ He shall call upon me, and I will answer him; I will be with him in trouble; I will deliver him and glorify him.

¹⁶ With long life I will satisfy him and show him my saving health.

57:2; 63:8). As indicated by verse 4, the shadow is an image of the safety to be found under the outstretched wings of the cherubim in the Holy of Holies. Almighty: literally, "Shaddai," an ancient name for God (see note on Ps 68:15).

c. Psalm 91:3 Snare of the fowler: a proverbial phrase for danger (see Ps 124:7; Prov 6:5; Hos 9:8).

d. Psalm 91:4 With his feathers he will shelter you: traditional biblical image (see note on Ps 17:8).

e. Psalm 91:5 Terror by night: resulting from true or false alerts of enemy attacks; attacks by day were announced by flying arrows.

f. Psalm 91:6 Pestilence... plague: dreaded mortal diseases that frequently grew into epidemics (see Deut 32:24; Hos 13:14; Hab 3:5). In place of the plague that lays waste at midday, other versions have: "devil at noon" or the "noonday devil" (apparently a mythological expression for a contagious disease presumed to be caused by the noonday sun).

g. Psalm 91:8 Your own eyes will behold: the righteous will be merely a spectator to the threats mentioned and not be harmed by them.

h. Psalm 91:11 These words were cited by Satan when tempting Christ to presumption against divine providence (Mt 4:6; Lk 4:10f).

i. Psalm 91:11 His angels: the teaching on guardian angels is common in the Old Testament (see Ps 34:7; Gen 24:7; Ex 23:20).

j. Psalm 91:12 Against a stone: along the stony paths of Canaan (see Ps 23:3).

k. Psalm 91:13 Asp . . . viper... lion . . . dragon: these terms correspond to the references found in verses 5-6 and complete the list of deadly threats against God's servants (see Am 5:19).

I. Psalm 91:14 The psalmist reinforces his message by utilizing the form of a prophetic oracle in which God promises Messianic blessings to all who put their trust in him (see Ps 50:15, 23; Rom 8:30).

m. Psalm 91:14 Raise high: i.e., "raise him to a high, safe place." My name: see note on Ps 5:12.

n. Psalm 91:15 The Lord gives assurance that his faithful will be honored for living honestly; they will enjoy themselves as his children in this life (see Pss 73:24; 112:9; 149:5; Isa 43:2; Jer 33:3).

o. Psalm 91:16 With a long life... my salvation: for the sages of Israel, a long life is the reward of the righteous (see Ex 23:26; Deut 4:40; 1 Sam 2:30; Job 5:26; Prov 3:2, 16; 10:27), crowned by salvation (see 1 Tim 4:8f).

詩篇 91

Chinese Union Version (Traditional)

91 住在至高者隱密處的，必住在全能者的蔭下。

2 我要論到耶和華說：他是我的避難所，是我的山寨,是我的神，是我所倚靠的。

3 他必救你脫離捕鳥人的網羅和毒害的瘟疫。

4 他必用自己的翎毛遮蔽你；你要投靠在他的翅膀底下；他的誠實是大 小的盾牌。

5 你必不怕黑夜的驚駭，或是白日飛的箭，

6 也不怕黑夜行的瘟疫，或是午間滅人的毒病。

7 雖有千人仆倒在你旁邊，萬人仆倒在你右邊，這災卻不得臨近你。

8 你惟親眼觀看，見惡人遭報。

9 耶和華是我的避難所；你已將至高者當你的居所，

10 禍患必不臨到你，災害也不挨近你的帳棚。

11 因他要為你吩咐他的使者，在你行的一切道路上保護你。

12 他們要用手托著你，免得你的腳碰在石頭上。

13 你要踹在獅子和虺蛇的身上，踐踏少壯獅子和大蛇。

14 神說：因為他專心愛我，我就要搭救他;因為他知道我的名,我要把他安置在高處。

15 他若求告我,我就應允他；他在急難中,我要與他同在；我要搭救他,使他尊貴。

16 我要使他足享長壽,將我的救恩顯明給他。

Psalm 91 Expanded Bible

Safe in the Lord

91 Those who go to God Most High for safety [ᴸdwell/sit in the shelter of God Most High]
   will be protected by [lodge in the shade/shadow of] the Almighty.

2 I will say to the LORD, "You are my place of safety [refuge] and protection [fortress].
   You are my God and I trust [have confidence in] you."

3 God will save [protect] you from hidden traps [ᴸthe snare of the fowler]
   and from deadly diseases [pestilence].

4 He will cover you with his feathers,
   and under his wings you can hide (will find refuge; <u>Deut. 32:11</u>; <u>Is. 31:5</u>; <u>Matt. 23:37</u>; <u>Luke 13:34</u>].
   His truth [faithfulness] will be your shield and protection [buckler; ᶜ a small shield].

5 You will not fear any danger by [terror at] night
   or an arrow that flies during the day.

6 You will not be afraid of diseases [ᴸ...or the pestilence] that come [walks; stalks] in the dark
   or sickness [ᴸstings] that strikes [devastates; overpowers] at noon.

7 At your side one thousand people may die [ᴸfall],
   or even ten thousand right beside you [hat your right hand],
   but you will not be hurt [ᴸit will not touch you].

8 You will only watch [ᴸlook with your eyes]
and see the wicked punished [recompensed].

9 The LORD is your protection [For you, LORD, are my refuge]; you have made God Most High your place of safety [dwelling place].

10 Nothing bad [evil; harmful] will happen to [befall] you;
   no .disaster [blow; or plague] will come to [approach] your home [ᴸtent].

11 He has put his angels in charge of [ᴸcommanded his angels/messengers concerning] you
   to watch over [keep; guard] you wherever you go [ᴸall your ways].

12 They will catch you [lift you up] in their hands

so that you will not hit your foot on a rock [Matt. 4:6; Luke 4:10–11].

13   You will walk [tread] on lions and cobras;
        you will step on [trample] strong lions and snakes.

14   The LORD says, "Whoever loves [desires] me, I will save [rescue].
    I will protect [lift to safety] those who know me [Lmy name].

15   They will call to me, and I will answer them.
        I will be with them in trouble [distress];
        I will rescue them and honor [glorify] them.

16   I will give them a long, full life [Lsatisfy them with length of days],
        and they will see how I can save [Lshow them my
salvation/victory]."

Psalm 91 New King James Version

Safety of Abiding in the Presence of God

91 He who dwells in the secret place of the Most High
Shall abide under the shadow of the Almighty.

2 I will say of the LORD, "He is my refuge and my fortress;
My God, in Him I will trust."

3 Surely He shall deliver you from the snare of the [a]fowler
And from the perilous pestilence.

4 He shall cover you with His feathers,
And under His wings you shall take refuge;
His truth shall be your shield and [b]buckler.

5 You shall not be afraid of the terror by night,
Nor of the arrow that flies by day,

6 Nor of the pestilence that walks in darkness,
Nor of the destruction that lays waste at noonday.

7 A thousand may fall at your side,
And ten thousand at your right hand;
But it shall not come near you.

8 Only with your eyes shall you look,
And see the reward of the wicked.

9 Because you have made the LORD, who is my refuge,
Even the Most High, your dwelling place,

10 No evil shall befall you,
Nor shall any plague come near your dwelling;

11 For He shall give His angels charge over you,
To keep you in all your ways.

12 In their hands they shall [c]bear you up,
Lest you [d]dash your foot against a stone.

13 You shall tread upon the lion and the cobra,
The young lion and the serpent you shall trample underfoot.

14 "Because he has set his love upon Me, therefore I will deliver him;
I will [e]set him on high, because he has known My name.

15   He shall call upon Me, and I will answer him;
      I will be with him in trouble;
      I will deliver him and honor him.
16   With [i]long life I will satisfy him,
      And show him My salvation."

Footnotes

a. <u>Psalm 91:3</u> One who catches birds in a trap or snare
b. <u>Psalm 91:4</u> A small shield
c. <u>Psalm 91:12</u> lift
d. <u>Psalm 91:12</u> strike
e. <u>Psalm 91:14</u> exalt him
f. <u>Psalm 91:16</u> Lit. length of days

Psalm 91 Wycliffe Bible

91 He that dwelleth in the help of the highest God; shall dwell in the protection of God of heaven. (He who dwelleth in the shelter of the Most High God, shall live under the protection of the God of heaven.)

[2] He shall say to the Lord, Thou art mine up-taker, and my refuge; my God, I shall hope in him. (He shall say to the Lord, Thou art my defender, and my refuge; my God, I trust in thee.)

[3] For he delivered me from the snare of hunters; and from a sharp word. (For he shall save me from the hunter's snare; and from a sharp word.)

[4] With his shoulders he shall make shadow to thee; and thou shalt have hope under his feathers. His truth shall (en) compass thee with a shield; (With his feathers he shall make a shadow for thee; and thou shalt have hope under his wings. His faithfulness shall surround thee like a shield.)

[5] thou shalt not dread of the night's dread. Of an arrow flying in the day, (Thou shalt not fear the terror in the night; nor an arrow flying in the day.)

[6] of a goblin going in darknesses; of assailing, and of a midday fiend. (Nor the pestilence going in darkness; nor the assailing of the plague at midday.)

[7] A thousand shall fall down from thy side, and ten thousand from thy right side; forsooth it shall not nigh to thee. (A thousand shall fall at thy side, and ten thousand at thy right side; but it shall not come even close to thee.)

[8] Nevertheless thou shalt behold with thine eyes; and thou shalt see the yielding of sinners. (Nevertheless thou shalt see with thine eyes; yea, thou shalt see the punishment of the sinners.)

[9] For thou, Lord, art mine hope; thou hast set thine help (to be the) alder-Highest. (For thou hast made the Lord to be thy hope; yea, the Most High to be thy help.)

10 Evil shall not come to thee; and a scourge shall not (come) nigh to thy tabernacle.

11 For God hath commanded to his angels of thee; that they keep thee in all thy ways. (For God hath commanded his angels to be all around thee; so that they keep thee safe on all thy ways.)

12 They shall bear thee in the hands; lest peradventure thou hurt thy foot at a stone. (They shall lift thee up with their hands; lest thou hurt thy foot on a stone.)

13 Thou shalt go upon a snake, and a cockatrice; and thou shalt defoul a lion, and a dragon (and thou shalt trample upon a lion, and a dragon).

14 (For God saith,) For he hoped in me, I shall deliver him (For God saith, Because he loved me. I shall save him); I shall defend him, for he knew my name.

15 He cried to me, and I shall hear him; I am with him in tribulation; I shall deliver him, and I shall glorify him. (When he crieth to me, I shall answer him; I shall be with him in all his troubles; I shall rescue him, and I shall honour him.)

16 I shall [ful]fill him with the length of days; and I shall show mine health to him. (I shall fulfill him with length of days, that is, with a long life; and I shall give my salvation, or my deliverance, to him/and I shall save him.)

Psalm 91 New International Version

Psalm 91

1   Whoever dwells in the shelter of the Most High
    will rest in the shadow of the Almighty,[a]

2   I will say of the LORD, "He is my refuge and my fortress,
    my God, in whom I trust."

3   Surely he will save you
    from the fowler's snare
    and from the deadly pestilence.

4   He will cover you with his feathers,
    and under his wings you will find refuge;
    his faithfulness will be your shield and rampart.

5   You will not fear the terror of night,
    nor the arrow that flies by day,

6   nor the pestilence that stalks in the darkness,
    nor the plague that destroys at midday.

7   A thousand may fall at your side,
    ten thousand at your right hand,
    but it will not come near you.

8   You will only observe with your eyes
    and see the punishment of the wicked.

9   If you say, "The LORD is my refuge,"
    and you make the Most High your dwelling,

10 no harm will overtake you,
    no disaster will come near your tent.

11 For he shall give his angels charge over thee,

to keep thee in all thy ways.

12 they will lift you up in their hands,

   so that you will not strike your foot against a stone.

13 You will tread on the lion and the cobra;

   you will trample the great lion and the serpent.

14 "Because he[b] loves me," says the LORD, "I will rescue him;

   I will protect him, for he acknowledges my name.

15 He will call on me, and I will answer him;

   I will be with him in trouble,

   I will deliver him and honor him.

16 With long life I will satisfy him

   and show him my salvation."

Footnotes

a. Psalm 91:1 Hebrew Shaddai

b. Psalm 91:14 That is, probably the king

Psalm 91 New International Reader's Version

Psalm 91

1   Whoever rests in the shadow of the Most High God
        will be kept safe by the Mighty One.

2   I will say about the LORD,
        "He is my place of safety.
    He is like a fort to me.
        He is my God. I trust in him."

3   He will certainly save you from hidden traps
        and from deadly sickness.

4   He will cover you with his wings.
        Under the feathers of his wings you will find safety.
        He is faithful. He will keep you safe like a shield or a tower.

5   You won't have to be afraid of the terrors that come during the night.
        You won't have to fear the arrows that come at you during the day.

6   You won't have to be afraid of the sickness that attacks in the
    darkness.
        You won't have to fear the plague that destroys at noon.

7   A thousand may fall dead at your side.
        Ten thousand may fall near your right hand.
        But no harm will come to you.

8   You will see with your own eyes
        how God punishes sinful people.

9   Suppose you say, "The LORD is the one who keeps me safe."
        Suppose you let the Most High God be like a home to you.

10   Then no harm will come to you.

No terrible plague will come near your tent.

11 The LORD will command his angels

to take good care of you.

12 They will lift you up in their hands.

Then you won't trip over a stone.

13 You will walk on lions and cobras.

You will crush mighty lions and poisonous snakes.

14 The LORD says, "I will save the one who loves me.

I will keep him safe, because he trusts in me.

15 He will call out to me, and I will answer him.

I will be with him in times of trouble.

I will save him and honor him.

16 I will give him a long and full life.

I will save him."

Psalm 91 New International Reader's Version

Psalm 91

1   Whoever rests in the shadow of the Most High God
    will be kept safe by the Mighty One.

2   I will say about the LORD,
    "He is my place of safety.
    He is like a fort to me.
    He is my God. I trust in him."

3   He will certainly save you from hidden traps
    and from deadly sickness.

4   He will cover you with his wings.
    Under the feathers of his wings you will find safety.
    He is faithful. He will keep you safe like a shield or a tower.

5   You won't have to be afraid of the terrors that come during the night.
    You won't have to fear the arrows that come at you during the day.

6   You won't have to be afraid of the sickness that attacks in the
    darkness.
    You won't have to fear the plague that destroys at noon.

7   A thousand may fall dead at your side.
    Ten thousand may fall near your right hand.
    But no harm will come to you.

8   You will see with your own eyes
    how God punishes sinful people.

9   Suppose you say, "The LORD is the one who keeps me safe."
    Suppose you let the Most High God be like a home to you.

10 Then no harm will come to you.

No terrible plague will come near your tent.

11 The LORD will command his angels

to take good care of you.

12 They will lift you up in their hands.

Then you won't trip over a stone.

13 You will walk on lions and cobras.

You will crush mighty lions and poisonous snakes.

14 The LORD says, "I will save the one who loves me.

I will keep him safe, because he trusts in me.

15 He will call out to me, and I will answer him.

I will be with him in times of trouble.

I will save him and honor him.

16 I will give him a long and full life.

I will save him."

Psalm 91 New International Version - UK

Psalm 91

1   Whoever dwells in the shelter of the Most High

       will rest in the shadow of the Almighty,[a]

2   I will say of the LORD, 'He is my refuge and my fortress,

       my God, in whom I trust.

3   Surely he will save you

       from the fowler's snare

       and from the deadly pestilence.

4   He will cover you with his feathers,

       and under his wings you will find refuge;

       his faithfulness will be your shield and rampart.

5   You will not fear the terror of night,

       nor the arrow that flies by day,

6   nor the pestilence that stalks in the darkness,

       nor the plague that destroys at midday.

7   A thousand may fall at your side,

       ten thousand at your right hand,

       but it will not come near you.

8   You will only observe with your eyes

       and see the punishment of the wicked.

9   If you say, 'The LORD is my refuge,'

       and you make the Most High your dwelling,

10   no harm will overtake you,

       no disaster will come near your tent.

11   For he will command his angels concerning you

to guard you in all your ways;

12 they will lift you up in their hands,

   so that you will not strike your foot against a stone.

13 You will tread on the lion and the cobra;

   you will trample the great lion and the serpent.

14 'Because he[b] loves me,' says the LORD, 'I will rescue him;

   I will protect him, for he acknowledges my name.

15 He will call on me, and I will answer him;

   I will be with him in trouble,

   I will deliver him and honour him.

16 With long life I will satisfy him

   and show him my salvation!'

Footnotes

a. <u>Psalm 91:1</u> Hebrew *Shaddai*

b. <u>Psalm 91:14</u> That is, probably the king

Psalm 91;1-16

91 Owo ekededi emi oduñde ke n d i̲ be ebiet Ata Edikon

Eyenyene itieidun ke mfụt Ata Okposoň.

2 Ami nyọdọhọ Jehovah nte: "Afo edi ebiet uboho mi ye ọkpọsọn ebiet mi,

Abasi mi, emi ndibuotde idem."

3 Koro enye ayanyaña fi osio ke afia omum inuen,

Osio ke udoño nsobo.

4 Enye ayada ntañ esie ofụk fi,

Afo oyonyun e d i̲ be ke idak mba esie.

Akpaniko esie eyedi akwa otuekọn ye ibibene ukpeme.

5 Afo udufeheke nkpondik ekededi ke okoneyo,

Mmê idan eke efede ke uwemeyo,

6 Mmê idiok udoño eke asañade ke ekim,

Mmê nsobo eke abiatde ke ufọt uwemeyo.

7 Owo tosin kiet ẹ ye d u ọ ñ ọ fi ke ñkañ

Tosin duop eyenyuñ ẹduọñọ ke ubok nnasia fị

Edi enye idisañake ikpere fi.

8 Afo edisese mmọ ke enyin kpọt

Onyun okut nte esiode mme idiokowo usiene.

9 Koro afo ọdohode ete: "Jehovah edi ebiet ubọhọ mi,"

Afo amanam Ata Edikoñ edi ebietidụñ fo;

10 Baba afanikon kiet idisimke fi,

Udoño idikam isañake ikpere tent fo.

11 Koro enye ọyọnọ mme angel esie ewụhọ abaña fi,

Man ekpeme fi ke kpukpru usụñ fo.

12 Mmọ ẹyekama fi ke ubọk mmọ,
   Mbak afo udutuak ukot fo ke itiat ekededi.

13 Afo ayanuak abak ayara ekpe ye ebre ke ikpat;
   Oyonyun edighi ekpe ye akamba urukikọt.

14 Koro enye amade mi,
   Ami ñko nyonọ enye edinyaña.
   Ami nyekpeme enye koro enye ofịdkde enyiñ mi.

15 Enye eyeseme okot mi, ndien ami nyeyere enye.
   Nyodu ye enye ke ini nnanenyin.
   Nyanyaña enye mnyụn nọ enye ubọñ.

16 Nyada ediwak usen nyuhọ enye,
   Nyonyuñ nnam enye okut edinyaña mi.

Kitap (Turkish Bible)

Mezmurlar 91

1 Yüceler Yücesinin barınağında oturan, Her Şeye Gücü Yetenin gölgesinde barınır.

2 ‹‹O benim sığınağım, kalemdir›› derim RAB için,

‹‹Tanrımdır, Ona güvenirim.››

3 Çünkü O seni avcı tuzağından, Ölümcül hastalıktan kurtarır.

4 Seni kanatlarının altına alır, Onların altına sığınırsın.

Onun sadakati senin kalkanın, siperin olur.

5 Ne gecenin dehşetinden korkarsın, Ne gündüz uçan oktan,

Ne karanlıkta dolaşan hastalıktan, Ne de öğleyin yok eden kırgından.

6 Ne gecenin dehşetinden korkarsın, Ne gündüz uçan oktan,

Ne karanlıkta dolaşan hastalıktan, Ne de öğleyin yok eden kırgından. 7 Yanında bin kişi,

Sağında on bin kişi kırılsa bile, Sana dokunmaz.

8 Sen yalnız kendi gözlerinle seyredecek,

Kötülerin cezasını göreceksin. 9 Sen RABbi kendine sığınak,

Yüceler Yücesini konut edindiğin için, 10 Başına kötülük gelmeyecek, Çadırına felaket yaklaşmayacak.

11 Çünkü Tanrı meleklerine buyruk verecek,

Gideceğin her yerde seni korusunlar diye.

12 Elleri üzerinde taşıyacaklar seni, Ayağın bir taşa çarpmasın diye.

13 Aslanın, kobranın üzerine basıp geçeceksin,

Genç aslanı, yılanı çiğneyeceksin. 14 ‹‹Beni sevdiği için

Onu kurtaracağım›› diyor RAB,

‹‹Beni iyi tanıdığı için Ona kale olacağım.

15 Bana seslenince onu yanıtlayacağım, Sıkıntıda onun yanında olacağım,

Kurtarıp yücelteceğim onu.

16 Onu uzun ömürle doyuracak,

Ona kurtarışımı göstereceğim.

New Revised Standard Version Updated Edition (NRSV-UE)

Psalm 91
Assurance of God's Protection

1 You who live in the shelter of the Most High,
   who abide in the shadow of the Almighty,[a]

2 will say to the Lord, "My refuge and my fortress;
   my God, in whom I trust."

3 For he will deliver you from the snare of the hunter
   and from the deadly pestilence;

4 he will cover you with his pinions,
   and under his wings you will find refuge;
   his faithfulness is a shield and defense.

5 You will not fear the terror of the night
   or the arrow that flies by day

6 or the pestilence that stalks in darkness
   or the destruction that wastes at noon-day.

7 A thousand may fall at your side,
   ten thousand at your right hand,
   but it will not come near you.

8 You will only look with your eyes
   and see the punishment of the wicked.

9 Because you have made the Lord your refuge,[b]
   the Most High your dwelling place,

10 no evil shall befall you,
   no scourge come near your tent.

11 For he will command his angels concerning you
     to guard you in all your ways.

12 On their hands they will bear you up,
     so that you will not dash your foot against a stone.

13 You will tread on the lion and the adder;
     the young lion and the serpent you will trample under foot.

14 Those who love me, I will deliver;
     I will protect those who know my name.

15 When they call to me, I will answer them;
     I will be with them in trouble;
     I will rescue them and honor them.
16 With long life I will satisfy them
     and show them my salvation.

Footnotes
91.1 Traditional rendering of Heb Shaddai
91.9 Cn: Heb Because you, Lord, are my refuge; you have made

Psalm 91 Tree of Life Version

Dwell in the Shelter of Elyon

Psalm 91

1   He who dwells in the shelter of Elyon,
    will abide in the shadow of Shaddai.

2   I will say of Adonai,
    "He is my refuge and my fortress,
        my God, in whom I trust.

3   For He will rescue you from the hunter's trap
    and from the deadly pestilence.

4   He will cover you with His feathers,
    and under His wings you will find refuge.
    His faithfulness is body armor and shield.

5   You will not fear the terror by night,
    nor the arrow that flies by day,

6   nor the plague that stalks in darkness,
        nor the scourge that lays waste at noon.

7   A thousand may fall at your side,
    and ten thousand at your right hand,
    but it will not come near you.

8   You will only look on with your eyes
    and see the wicked paid back.

9   For you have made Elyon your dwelling,
    even ADONAI, who is my refuge,

10 so no evil will befall you
    nor any plague come near your tent.

11 For He will give His angels charge over you,

to guard you in all your ways.

12   Upon their hands they will lift you up,
lest you strike your foot against a stone.[a]

13   You will tread upon the lion and cobra,
trample the young lion and serpent.

14   "Because he has devoted his love to Me,
    I will deliver him.
I will set him securely on high,
    because he knows My Name.

15   When he calls on Me, I will answer him.
I will be with him in trouble, rescue him, and honor him.

16   With long life will I satisfy him
and show him My salvation."

Footnotes

a.   Psalm 91:12 cf. Matt. 4:6; Luke 4:10-11

Thai Holy Bible

Psalms / สดุดี 91

1 ผู้ที่อาศัยอยู่ ณ ที่กำบังขององค์ผู้สูงสุดจะอยู่ในร่มเงาของผู้ทรงมหิทธิฤทธิ์

2 ข้าพเจ้าจะกล่าวถึงพระเยโฮวาห์ว่า 'พระองค์ทรงเป็นที่ลี้ภัยของข้าพระองค์และป้อมปราการของข้าพระองค์ พระเจ้าของข้าพระองค์ ผู้ที่ข้าพระองค์จะไว้วางใจ"

3 เพราะพระองค์จะทรงช่วยตัวท่านให้พ้นจากกับของพรานนกและจากโรคภัยอย่างร้ายแรงนั้น

4 พระองค์จะทรงปกท่านไว้ด้วยปีกของพระองค์ และท่านจะวางใจอยู่ใต้ปีกของพระองค์ ความจริงของพระองค์เป็นโล่และเป็นดั้งของท่าน

5 ท่านจะไม่กลัวความสยดสยอง ในกลางคืน หรือกลัวลูกธนูที่ปลิวไปในกลางวัน

6 หรือโรคภัยที่ไล่มาในความมืด หรือความพินาศที่เกิดความหายนะในเที่ยงวัน

7 พันคนจะล้มอยู่ที่ข้างๆท่าน หมื่นคนที่มือขวาของท่าน แต่ภัยนั้นจะไม่มาใกล้ท่าน

8 ท่านจะมองดูด้วยตาท่านนั้น และเห็นการตอบแทนแก่คนชั่ว

9 เพราะท่านได้กระทำ ให้พระเยโฮวาห์ผู้เป็นที่ลี้ภัยของข้าพเจ้าคืององค์ผู้สูงสุด เป็นที่อยู่ของท่าน

10 ไม่มีการร้าย ใดๆตกมาบนท่าน ไม่มีภัยมาใกล้ที่อาศัยของท่าน

11 เพราะพระองค์จะรับสั่งเหล่าทูตสวรรค์ของพระองค์ ในเรื่องท่าน ให้ระแวดระวังท่านในทางทั้งปวงของท่าน

12 เขาทั้งหลายจะเอามือประคองชูท่านไว้ เกรงว่าเท้าของท่านจะกระแทกหิน

13 ท่านจะเหยียบสิงโตและงูเห่า ท่านจะย่ำสิงโตหนุ่มและมังกร

14 เพราะเขาผูกพันกับเราด้วยความรัก เราจึงจะช่วยเขาให้พ้น เราจะตั้งเขาไว้ในที่สูง เพราะเขารู้จักนามของเรา

15 เขาจะร้องทูลเรา และเราจะตอบเขา เราจะอยู่กับเขาในยามลำบาก เราจะช่วยเขาให้พ้นและให้เกียรติเขา

16 เราจะให้เขาอิ่มใจด้วยชีวิตยืนยาว และสำแดงความรอดของเราแก่เขา

Tagalog Holy Bible

Mga Awit 91

1 Siyang tumatahan sa lihim na dako ng Kataastaasan. Ay mananatili sa lilim ng Makapangyarihan sa lahat

2 Aking sasabihin tungkol sa Panginoon, siya'y aking kanlungan at aking katibayan, ang Dios ko na siyang aking tinitiwalaan.

3 Sapagka't kaniyang ililigtas ka sa silo ng paninilo, at sa mapamuksang salot.

4 Kaniyang tatakpan ka ng kaniyang mga bagwis, at sa ilalim ng kaniyang mga pakpak ay manganganlong ka: ang kaniyang katotohanan ay kalasag at baluti.

5 Ikaw ay hindi matatakot sa kakilabutan sa gabi, ni sa pana man na humihilagpos kung araw;

6 Dahil sa salot na dumarating sa kadiliman, ni dahil sa paggiba man na sumisira sa katanghaliang tapat.

7 Isang libo ay mabubuwal sa iyong siping, at sangpung libo sa iyong kanan; nguni't hindi lalapit sa iyo.

8 Iyong mamamasdan lamang ng iyong mga mata, at iyong makikita ang ganti sa masama.

9 Sapagka't ikaw, Oh Panginoon, ay aking kanlungan! Iyong ginawa ang Kataastaasan na iyong tahanan;

10 Walang kasamaang mangyayari sa iyo, ni anomang salot ay lalapit sa iyong tolda.

11 Sapagka't siya'y magbibilin sa kaniyang mga anghel tungkol sa iyo, upang ingatan ka sa lahat ng iyong mga lakad.

12 Kanilang dadalhin ka sa kanilang mga kamay, baka matisod ka ng iyong paa sa isang bato.

13 Iyong yayapakan ang leon at ang ulupong: ang batang leon at ang ahas ay yuyurakan mo ng iyong mgapaa.

14 Sapagka't kaniyang inilagak ang kaniyang pagibig sa akin, kaya't iniligtas ko siya: aking ilalagay siya sa mataas, sapagka't kaniyang naalaman ang pangalan ko.

15 Siya'y tatawag sa akin, at sasagutin ko siya; ako'y sasa kaniya sa kabagabagan: aking ililigtas siya, at pararangalan siya.

16 Aking bubusugin siya ng mahabang buhay, at ipakikita ko sa kaniya ang aking pagliligtas.

Biblia Takatifu – Swahili Bible

Zaburi Psalms 91

1 Aketiye mahali pa siri pake Aliye juu Atakaa katika uvuli wake Mwenyezi.

2 Nitasema, Bwana ndiye kimbilio langu na ngome yangu, Mungu wangu nitakayemtumaini.

3 Maana Yeye atakuokoa na mtego wa mwindaji, Na katika tauni iharibuyo.4 Kwa manyoya yake atakufunika, Chini ya mbawa zake utapata kimbilio; Uaminifu wake ni ngao na kigao.

5 Hutaogopa hofu ya usiku, Wala mshale urukao mchana,

6 Wala tauni ipitayo gizani, Wala uele uharibuo adhuhuri,

7 Ijapo watu elfu waanguka ubavuni pako. Naam, kumi elfu mkono wako wa kuume! Hata hivyo hautakukaribia wewe.

8 Ila kwa macho yako utatazama, Na kuyaona malipo ya wasio haki.

9 Kwa kuwa Wewe Bwana ndiwe kimbilio langu; Umemfanya Aliye juu kuwa makao yako.

10 Mabaya hayatakupata wewe, Wala tauni haitaikaribia hema yako.

11 Kwa kuwa atakuagizia malaika zake Wakulinde katika njia zako zote.

12 Mikononi mwao watakuchukua, Usije ukajikwaa mguu wako katika jiwe.

13 Utawakanyaga simba na nyoka, Mwana-simba na joka utawaseta kwa miguu.

14 Kwa kuwa amekaza kunipenda Nitamwokoa; na kumweka palipo juu, kwa kuwa amenijua Jina langu.

15 Ataniita nami nitamwitikia; Nitakuwa pamoja naye taabuni, Nitamwokoa na kumtukuza;

16 Kwa siku nyingi nitamshibisha, Nami nitamwonyesha wokovu wangu.

Муқаддас Китоб (UZB)

Psalms/Забур / Zabur 91

1 Сано. Шаббат куни айтилган қўшиқ.

2 Эй Эгам, Сенга шукур айтмоқ яхшидир, Эй Худойи Таоло, Сенга ҳамду сано куйламоқ яхшидир.

3 Эълон қилмоқ яхшидир субҳидамда содиқ севгингни, Эълон қилмоқ яхшидир кечалари садоқатингни.

4 Яхшидир айтмоқ буларни мусиқа чалибЎн торли асбобда, лирада, арфа жўрлигида!

5 Эй Эгам, қудратли ишларингдан мен шодман, Қилган ишларингдан хурсанд бўлиб куйлайман.

6 Эй Эгам, ишларинг нақадар буюкдир! Ўйларинг жуда ҳам терандир!

7 Ақлсиз кимса буни била олмайди, Аҳмоқ кимса буни тушуна олмайди:

8 Гарчи фосиқлар майса каби униб чиқса ҳам, Бадкирдорлар гуллаб-яшнаса ҳам, Улар то абад йўқ бўлади.

9 Сен-чи, эй Эгам, то абад улуғворсан.

10 Эй Эгам, душманларинг албатта йўқ бўлади, Улар шубҳасиз ҳалок бўлади. Бадкирдорларнинг ҳаммаси тарқалиб кетади.

11 Мени ёввойи буқадай кучли қилдинг, Қудратинг билан менга қайтадан куч ато этдинг.

12 Душманларим мағлубиятин кўзларим кўрди, Бадкирдорлар заволин қулоқларим эшитди.

13 Солиҳлар пальма дарахтидай гуллаб-яшнайди, Лубнондаги садр дарахтидай юксалади.

14 Улар Эгамизнинг уйига ўтқазилган, Худойимизнинг ҳовлисида улар яшнайди.

15 Кексаликда ҳам ҳамон ҳосил беради, Ям-яшил, навқирон бўлиб тураверади.

16 Улар биргаликда шундай деб эълон қилади: "Эгамиз одилдир! У менинг суянган қоямдир, Унда ноҳақлик йўқдир."

Xhosa Holy Bible

IiNdumiso 91

1 Ohleli esitheni IOsenyangweni, Azilalise emthunzini kaSomandla,

2 Uthi kuYehova, Hlathi lam, Mboniselo yam, Thixo wam, endikholose ngaye!

3 Ngokuba ngokwakhe uya kukuhlangula emgibeni womthiyeli, Endyikityeni yokufa eyeyelisayo.

4 Wokugubungela ngeentsiba zakhe, Uzimele phantsi kwamaphiko akhe. Likhaka, yingweletshetshe inyaniso yakhe.

5 Akuyi koyikiswa zizothuso ebusuku, Nalutolo lubaleka emini;

6 Nandyikitya yakufa ihamba esithokothokweni, Nasifo sibhubhisayo, sibhuqa emini enkulu.

7 Kungawa iwaka ecaleni kwakho, Isigidi ngasekunene kwakho, Kodwa kungasondeli nto kuwe.

8 Wokhangela ngamehlo akho odwa, Ukubonele ukubuyekezwa kwabangendawo.

9 Ngokuba nguwe, Yehova, ihlathi lam. Umenze Osenyangweni ikhaya lakho.

10 Akuyi kuqubisana bubi nawe. Kungafiki sibetho ententeni yakho.

11 Ngokuba izithunywa zakhe uziwisele umthetho ngawe, Ukuba zikugcine ezindleleni zakho zonke.

12 Zokuthwala wena ngezandla zozibini, Hleze ubetheke ngonyawo Iwakho etyeni.

13 Wonyathela phezu kwengonyama nephimpi, Uyinyashe ingonyama entsha nenamba ngeenyawo.

14 Ngokuba enamathele kum, ndomsiza; Ndimse engxondeni, ngokuba elazi igama lam.

15 Wondibiza, ndiphendule, Ndoba naye embandezelweni; Ndomhlangula, ndimzukise;

16 Ndimanelise ngemihla emide, Ndimbonise ukusindisa kwam.

Kitab Suci

JABUR 91

1 Anu nyalindung ka Nu Maha Agung, anu aya dina pangraksa Nu Maha Kawasa,

2 bisa unjukan ka Mantenna, "Gusti teh benteng panyalindungan abdi, Allah pangharepan abdi."

3 Mantenna baris ngajaga anjeun tina bahya nu teu tembong, tina panyakit anu mateni.

4 Mantenna baris mindingan anjeun ku jangjang-Na, anjeun baris aman dina pangraksa-Na, baris dijaga jeung ditangtayungan ku kasatiaana-Na.

5 Ti peuting teu kudu mingsir sieun balahi, ti beurang teu kudu rempan ku bahaya ngadadak.

6 Teu kudu risi ku panyakit nu datangna waktu poek, teu kudu rentag ku ajal anu narajang waktu caang beurang.

7 Najan sarebu anu rebah di gigireun, sapuluh rebu di sakurilingeun, anjeun mah moal kieu-kieu.

8 Ku anjeun bakal katingal, kumaha siksaanana jelema jahat.

9 Sabab nya Pangeran nu ku anjeun dijieun panyalindungan, nya Nu Maha Agung nu ku anjeun dipake panyaluuhan.

10 Anu matak, bahya moal aya anu datang, kaniaya moal aya nu nyampeurkeun ka eusi imah anjeun.

11 Allah baris nempatkeun malaikat-malaikat-Na, ngajaga anjeun sanajan aya di mana.

12 Ku eta anjeun teh ditaranggeuy, sangkan suku anjeun teu ngagasruk kana batu.

13 Singa galak jeung oray matih geku anjeun baris bisa ditincakan.

14 Allah ngandika, "Jalma nu nyaah ka Kamitangtu ku Kami disina salamet. Anu ngaku yen Kami teh Pangerantangtu ku Kami ditangtayungan.

15 Ana maranehna nyambat ka Kami tangtu dibales. Ana maranehna kasusahan, tangtu ku Kami dibaturan, tangtu ditulungan jeung dibere kahormatan.

16 Umurna rek dipanjangkeun, ku Kami rek disalametkeun."

Somali Holy Bible

SABUURRADII 91

1 Kan dega Ilaaha ugu sarreeya meeshiisa qarsoon Wuxuu joogi doonaa hooska Qaadirka.

2 Waxaan Rabbiga ka odhan doonaa, Isagu waa magangalkayga iyo qalcaddayda Oo waa Ilaahayga aan isku halleeyo.

3 Waayo, wuxuu kaa samatabbixin doonaa dabinka ugaadhsadaha, Iyo belaayada aad u xun.

4 Oo wuxuu kugu dedi doonaa baalashiisa, Oo waxaad magangeli doontaa baadadkiisa, Runtiisuna waxay tahay gaashaan iyo gabbaad.

5 Waa inaanad ka cabsan naxdinta habeennimada, Iyo fallaadha dharaarnimada duulaysa toona,

6 Ama belaayada gudcurka ku socota, Iyo halligaadda duhurka wax baabbi'isa.

7 Dhinacaaga waxaa ku dhici doona kun, Midigtaadana waxaa ku ag dhici doona toban kun, Innabase kuuma soo dhowaan doonto.

8 Laaklinse indhaha uun baad ku fiirin doontaa, Oo waxaad arki doontaa kuwa sharka leh abaalgudkooda.

9 Waayo, waxaad tidhi, Rabbigu waa magangalkayga, Oo Kan ugu sarreeya ayaa degmadayda ah.

10 Shar kuguma dhici doono, Belaayona teendhadaada uma soo dhowaan doonto.

11 Waayo, isagu wuxuu malaa'igihiisa ku amri doonaa Inay jidadkaaga oo dhan kugu ilaaliyaan.

12 Oo iyaguna gacmahooday sare kuugu qaban doonaan Inaanay cagtaadu dhagax ku dhicin.

13 Libaaxa iyo jilbiska ayaad ku joogsan doontaa, Oo waxaad ku tuman doontaa aaran libaax iyo abeesada.

14 Rabbigu wuxuu yidhi, Isagu aad buu ii jeclaaday, oo sidaas daraaddeed ayaan u samatabbixin doonaa, Meel sare ayaan ku fadhiisin doonaa, maxaa yeelay, magacayguu yiqiin.

15 Wuu i baryi doonaa, oo waan u jawaabi doonaa, Oo markuu dhibaataysan yahay, waan la jiri doonaa, Oo wwaan samatabbixin doonaa, waanan murwayn doonaa.

16 Cimri dheer ayaan ka dhergin doonaa, Oo waxaan tusi doonaa badbaadintayda.

Chráskov prevod

Psalmi 91

1 Kdor stanuje v zavetju Najvišjega, bo počival v senci Vsemogočnega.

2 Zato pravim Gospodu: Pribežališče si moje ingrad moj, Bog moj, v katerega upam.

3 Kajti on te bo rešil iz zanke ptičarjeve in kuge pogubne.

4 S perutjo svojo te pokrije, in pod krili njegovimi ti bo zavetje, ščit in bran je resnica njegova.

5 Ne boj se nočnega strahu, ne pšice, ki šviga po dnevi,

6 ne pogube, ki lazi v temi, ne kuge, ki razsaja opoldne.

7 Pade jih ob strani tvoji tisoč in desetkrat tisoč na desnici tvoji, a k tebi se ne približa.

8 Samo z očmi svojimi boš to gledal in videl povračilo brezbožnikov.

9 Ker si rekel: Ti, Gospod, si pribežališče moje, Najvišjega si postavil za prebivališče svoje,

10 ne zadene te nesreča nobena in šiba se ne približa šotoru tvojemu.

11 Zakaj angelom svojim zapove zate, da te hranijo po vseh potih tvojih.

12 Na rokah te bodo nosili, da ne zadeneš z nogo svojo ob kamen.

13 Po divjem levu boš hodil in po kači, teptal boš leva mladiča in zmaja.

14 Ker mi je vdan v ljubezni, pravi Bog, ga hočem oteti; na varno ga postavim, ker pozna ime moje.

15 Kadar me zakliče, ga uslišim, na strani mu bodem v stiski; rešim ga in počastim.

16 Nasitim ga z dolgostjo življenja in storim, da z veseljem gleda zveličanje moje.

Sinhala Holy Bible

Psalms / ගීතාවලිය 91

1 මහ ෝේත්ත3යB හB ර ස්ස්ථානහයනි වසන
තැනැන්හත් සර්වපරානුයායB හේ බසවාසයකරB හB ය.

2 උB ව B හස් මාහෝ රක්ෂාස්ථානයය, මාහෝ ශකාටුවය; මා
විසB B විශ්වාසකරන මාහෝ හෙවියB ව B හස්ය A ස්වාමී B
ැන කියB හනම්,

3 ඔක්පීසා ෙ උB ව B හස් පක්ෂී වැහේ මලුපති B ෙ
විනාශකරන වශහයB ෙ සිද්ධ මුෙ රිනක,

4 උB ව B හස් ස්වකීය පියාපති B 80 වසක, ඔබ දුB ව
B හස්B පියාපන් යට ආරක්ෂාවB හනහිය, උB ව B හස්හේ
සනසවාදිකම පලි ක්ය, ම ාපලි ක්ය.

5 රාත්රිහේ හීනියටවත්, ෙවාහේ විදින ඊගසටවත්,

6 අළුහර් යන විසංගතයB, ඉරමුඩුB හේ පායකරන
විනාශයටවත්
30 හය හනාවණීය.

7 ඔහේ පැත්තක ෙ ෙ සක්ෙ ෙකුණු තB හී ෙස සB ෙ
වැහටB හනෝය; එහ න් එය සිබධ පං හනාවB නB ය.

8 නිබී ඇස්වත් බෑ දුෂ්ටයාහේ විපාතය ෙකිනවා පස්සක්ය.

9 ඒ පික්පීසා ෙ ස්වාඩී, ඔබ හේ
රක්ෂාස්ථානයය, ඔබ මහ ෝේත්තමයාණB
ඔහේ වාසස්ථානය කරගහිය;

10 ඔබට කිසි පරB ඉනාපෑමියයB හB ය, ඔහේ
කුඩාරමට විසං හයක් පං හනාවB හB ය,

11 මක්පීසා ෙ 80 සියලු මාර්ගවලදී ඔබ
ආරක්ෂාකරන පිණිස උB ව B හස් ස්වකීය දුනයB ට
ඔබ ගැන අඥනභෘක්ක,

12 ශ්ඕ ඔහේ පය හලක හනාවදින පිණිස ඔවුBහේ අත් පිට ඔබ උසුලා ය,

13 ශ්ේසිං යාB හපාෙකාත් පාගනහිය, කරුණා සිං යාක් සර්පයාන් පAB පාසනA.

14 ඉ මා හකහරණි ඇනුවූ බැවිB ඉ මුෙො රිBහනම්. 8Bහේ නාමය ෙොෙක සිටින බැවිB ඉ උසස් කරd,

15 ඉ මට යාකරEහBය, මෙම උත්තරහොBහනම්; දුරැදි ඉ සමයා සිටිනම්, ඉ මුෙො හකහරවයට පමුණුවBh,

16 දිර්සායුෂහයB ඉ සැජීමට පසුණුවා, මාහේ සැළවීම ඉට ෙක්වBහනA.

Romanian Holy Bible

Psalmi 91

1 Celce stă supt ocrotirea Celui Prea Inalt, şi se odihneşte la umbra Celui Atoputernic,

2 zice despre Domnul:,,El este locul meu de scăpare, şi cetăţula mea, Dumnezeul meu în care mă încred!"

3 Da, El te scapă de latul vinătorului, de ciumă şi de pustiirile ei.

4 El te va acoperi cu penele Lui, şi te vei ascunde supt aripile Lui. Căci scut şi pavăză este credincioşia Lui!

5 u trebuie să te temi nici de groaza din timpul nopţii, nici de săgeata care sboară ziua,

6 nici de ciuma, care umblă în întunerec, nici de molima, care bintuie ziua nameaza mare.

7 mie să cadă alături de tine, şi zece mii la dreapta ta, dar de tine nu se va apropia.

8 Doar vei privi cu ochii, şi vei vedea răsplătirea celor răi.

9 Pentrucă zici:,,Domnul este locul meu de adăpost! şi faci din Cel Prea Inalt turnul tău de scăpare,

10 de aceea nici o nenorocire nu te va ajunge, nici o urgie nu se va apropia de cortul tău.

11 Căci El va porunci îngerilor săi să te păzească în toate căile tale;

12 şi ei te vor duce pe mini, ca nu cumva să-ţi loveşti piciorul de vreo piatră.

13 Vei păşi peste lei şi peste năpirci, şi vei călca peste pui de lei şi peste şerpl..

14,,Fiindcă Mă iubeşte-zice Domnul-deaceea il voi izbăvi; il voi ocroti, căci cunoaşte Numele Meu.

15 Cind Mă va chema, ii voi răspunde; voi fi cu el in strimtorare, il voi izbăvi şi-l voi proslavi

16 il voi sătura cu viaţă lungă, şi-i voi arăta mintuirea Mea

Norwegian Holy Bible

Salmenes 91

1 Den som sitter i den Høiestes skjul, som bor i den Allmektiges skygge,

2 han sier til Herren: Min tilflukt og min borg, min Gud som jeg setter min lit til!

3 For han frir dig av fuglefangerens snare, fra ødeleggende pest.

4 Med sine vingefjærer dekker han dig, og under hans vinger finner du ly; hans trofasthet er skjold og vern.

5 Du skal ikke frykte for nattens redsler, for pil som flyver om dagen,

6 for pest som farer frem i mørket, for sott som ødelegger om middagen.

7 Faller tusen ved din side og ti tusen ved din høire hånd, til dig skal det ikke nå.

8 Du skal bare skue det med dine øine, og se hvorledes de ugudelige får sin lønn.

9 For du, Herre, er min tilflukt. Den Høieste har du gjort til din bolig;

10 intet ondt skal vederfares dig, og ingen plage skal komme nær til ditt telt.

11 For han skal gi sine engler befaling om dig at de skal bevare dig på alle dine veier.

12 De skal bære dig på hendene, forat du ikke skal støte din fot på nogen sten.

13 På løve og huggorm skal du trå; du skal trå ned unge løver og slanger.

14 For han henger fast ved mig, og jeg vil utfri ham; jeg vil føre ham i sikkerhet, for han kjenner mitt navn.

15 Han skal påkalle mig, og jeg vil svare ham; jeg er med ham i nøden, jeg vil utfri ham og føre ham til ære.

16 Med et langt liv vil jeg mette ham og la ham skue min frelse.

Latvijas Bībeles Biedrība (LTV 1965)

Psalmi 91

1 Kas dzīvo Visaugstākā patvērumā un mīt Visuvarenā ēnā,

2 Tas saka uz to Kungu: „Mans patvērums un mana pils, mans Dievs, uz ko es pajaujos!"

3 Jo Viņš tevi glābj kā putnu no ķērēja cilpas, pasargā no iznīcinātāja mēja.

4 Viņš tevi sedz ar saviem spārniem, zem Viņa spārniem tu esi paglābts; Viņa patiesība ir tavs vairogs un brupas.

5 Tu nebisties nakts briesmu nedz ari bultu, kas dienu skraida,

6 Nedz mēra, kas tumsā lien, nedz sērgu, kas pusdienā nomaitā.

7 Jebšu tūkstoši krīt tev blakus un desmit tūkstoši tev pa labo roku, taču tevi tas neskars.

8 Tiešām, tu vēl skatīsi ar savām acīm un redzēsi, kā bezdievjiem tiek atmaksāts.

9 Tiešām, Tu, ak Kungs, esi mans patvērums 1 Visuaugstāko tu (dziesminieks pats) esi izraudzījis sev par aizsargu.

10 Nekāds Jaunums tev nenotiks, nedz kāda nediena tuvosies tavai teltij,

11 Jo Viņš sūtīs tev savus eņģeļus tevi pasargāt visos tavos ceļos.

12 Viņi tevi uz rokām nesīs, lai tava kāja nepieduras pie akmens.

13 Pār lauvām un odzēm tu varēsi staigāt, tu samiņi jaunos lauvas un čūskas!

14 „Tādēļ, ka viņš Man stipri pie-ķēries, Es viņu izglābšu; Es viņu paaugstināšu, jo viņš pazīst manu vārdu.

15 Kad viņš mani piesauks, tad Es viņu paklausīšu; Es viņam esmu klāt bēdās, Es viņu izraušu no tām un celšu godā.

Kannada Holy Bible

1 ಮಹೋನ್ನ ತನ್ ಮರೆಯಾದ ಸ್ಥ ಳದಲ್ಲಿ ಹ್ಮು ಸ್ವವಶಕ್ತ ನ್ ನೆರಳಿನ್ಲಿ ತಂಗುವನು.

2 ನ್ನ ಆಶ್ರ ಯವೂ ಕೋಟೆಯೂ ನಾನು ಹೈಧ್ಮ ನ್ನ ದೇವರೂ ಎಂದು ನಾನು ಕ್ರವನಿಗೆ ಹೇಳುತ್ತ ರೋನೆ.

3 ನಿಶ್ಚ ಯವಾಗಿ ಆತನು ನಿನ್ನ ನುನ ಬೇಡನ್ ಅಲ್ಪವಿಲೂ ಅಪಾಯದ ಜಾಡಯ ದಂದಲೂ ಬಿಡಿಸು ವನು,

4 ತನ್ನ ರೆಕ್ಕೆ ಗಳಿಂದ ನಿನ್ನ ನುನ ಹವಿಸವನುತ್ತಲೆಕ್ಕೆ ಗಳ ಕ್ಳಗೆ ಆಶ್ರ ಯಿಸಿಕಳು ವಿ; ಆತನ್ ಸ್ತಯ ವು ನಿನ್ನ ಬೇಡವೂ ದಾಲೂ ಆಗಿದೆ.

5 ರಾತ್ರ ಯ ಭಯಂಕ್ರತ್ಮೂ ಹಗಲಲ್ಲಿ ಹಾರುವ ಚ್ಮ

6 ಅಂಧಕಾರದಲ್ಲಿ ನ್ನೆಯುವ ಜಾಡಯ ಕ್ಕೆ ಇಲಿವೆಮಧ್ಯಯ ಹವ ದಲ್ಲಿ ಹಾಳು ಮಾಡುವ ನಾಡನ್ಕ್ಕ ನಿೋನು ಭಯಪಡದೆ ಇರುವಿ,

7 ನಿನ್ನ ಕ್ಡೆಯಲ್ಲಿ ಸಾವಿರ ಜನ್ಮೂ ನಿನ್ನ ಡ್ಮಿ ಹತ್ತ ಸಾವಿರ ಜನ್ಮೂ ಬಿದ್ದಾ ಗೂಯ ನಿನ್ನ ಸ್ಕಿಂಿಪಕ್ಕೆ ಅದು ಬರುವದಲಿ .

8 ನಿನ್ನ ಕ್ಣ್ಣ ಗಳಿಂದ ಮಾತರ ನಿೋನು ದೃಷ್ಟಿ ಸಿ ಡಶ್ ರಿಗೆ ಮುಖ್ಯಯ ಗೆ ಮುಯಯಯಲಾಗುವದನುನ ನೋಡುವಿ.

9 ಮಹೋನ್ನ ತನಾದ ಕ್ರವನ್ನುನ ಸ್ಮಿಆಲಯ ವಾಗಿಯೂ ನಿವಾಸ್ಥಾಥ ನ್ಮಾಗಿಯೂ ಮಾಡಿಕಂಡ ದಾ ರಿಂದ

10 ಕೇಡು ನಿನ್ನ ನುನ ಮುಟ್ಕಿ ದು; ಯಾವ ವ್ಯಾಧ್ಯಿಯೂ ನಿನ್ನ ನಿವಾಸ್ಕ್ಕೆಸ್ಕಿಪಿಸುದ್ಮ.

11 ನಿನ್ನ ಎಲ್ಲಿ ಮಾರ್ಗವಗಳಲ್ಲಿ ನಿನ್ನ ನುನ ಕಾಕ್ಕ ಆತನು ತನ್ನದೂತರಿಗೆ ನಿನ್ನ ವಿಷ್ಯವಾಗಿ ಆಜ್ಞಾ ಪಿಸುವನು.

12 ನಿನ್ನ ಪಾದವು ಕ್ಲಿ ಗೆ ತಗಲದ ಹಾಗೆ ಅವರು ನ್ನಿನನ ತಮಮ ಕೈಗಳಲ್ಲಿಎತ್ತ ಕಳು ವರು.

13 ಸಿಂಹ ಸ್ಪವ ಮೇಲೆ ನ್ಡೆಯುವಿ; ಯಕ್ಕೌ ಸಿಂಹವನ್ನನಘಟ್ಟಪ್ಪವವನ್ಮನ ತ್ಳಿದು ಬಿಡುವಿ.

14 ಅವನು ತನ್ನ ಹಿ ರೋತ್ರಯನುನ ನ್ನ ಮೇಲೆ ಇಟ್ಟಿ ದ್ದಾ ನೆ; ಅದದರಿಂದ ಅವನುನ ತಪಿತಿ ಸುವೇನು; ಅವನು ನ್ನ ಹೆಸ್ರನುನ ತ್ಳಿದರುವದರಿಂದ ಅವನ್ಮನ ಉನ್ನ ತ್ಳ್ಳಿ ಡುವೇನು.

15 ಅವನು ನ್ನ ನನ ಕ್ರೆಯುವನು; ನಾನು ಅಯೇಉತ ರ ಕಡುವೇನು; ಇಕ್ಕ್ ಟ್ಟಿ ನ್ಲ್ಲಿ ನಾನು ಅವನ್ ಸಂಗಡ ಇದೂ ಅವನ್ಮನ ತಪಿತಿ ಸಿ; ಘನಪಡಿಸುವೇನು.

16 ದೆಾ ಲ ವಯುಷ್ಟ ದಂದ ಅವನ್ಮನ ತ್ಳಿತ ಹ್ಮ್ನ ರಕ್ಷಣೆಯನುನಅವನಿಗೆ ತೋರಿಸುವೇನು.

Japanese Holy Bible – Kuogo-yaku

Psalms /詩編91

1 いと高き者のもとにある隠れ場に住む人、全能者の陰にやどる人は

2 主に言うであろう、「わが避け所、わが城、わが信頼しまつるわが神」と。

3 主はあなたをかりゅうどのわなと、恐ろしい疫病から助け出されるからである。

4 主はその羽をもって、あなたをおおわれる。あなたはその翼の下に避け所を得るであろう。そのまことは大盾、また小盾である。

5 あなたは夜の恐ろしい物をも、昼に飛んでくる矢をも恐れることはない。

6 また暗やみに歩きまわる疫病をも、真昼に荒す滅びをも恐れることはない。

7 たとい千人はあなたのかたわらに倒れ、万人はあなたの右に倒れても、その災はあなたに近づくことはない。

8 あなたはただ、その目をもって見、悪しき者の報いを見るだけである。

9 あなたは主を避け所とし、いと高き者をすまいとしたので、

10 災はあなたに臨まず、悩みはあなたの天幕に近づくことはない。

11 これは主があなたのために天使たちに命じて、あなたの歩むすべての道であなたを守らせられるからである。

12 彼らはその手で、あなたをささえ、石に足を打ちつけることのないようにする。

13 あなたはししと、まむしとを踏み、若いししと、へびとを足の下に踏みにじるであろう。

14 彼はわたしを愛して離れないゆえに、わたしは彼を助けよう。彼はわが名を知るゆえに、わたしは彼を守る。

15 彼がわたしを呼ぶとき、わたしは彼に答える。わたしは彼の悩みのときに、共にいて、彼を救い、彼に光栄を与えよう。

16 わたしは長寿をもって彼を満ち足らせ、わが救を彼に示すであろう。

Korean Holy bible

Psalms / 시편 91

1 지존자의 은밀한 곳에 거하는 자는 전능하신 자의 그늘
아래 거하리로다

2 내가 여호와를 가리켜 말하기를 저는 나의 피난처요 나의
요새요 나의 의뢰하는 하나님이라 하리니

3 이는 저가 너를 새 사냥군의 올무에서와 극한 염병에서
건지실 것임이로다

4 저가 너를 그 깃으로 덮으시리니 네가 그 날개 아래 피하리로다
그의 진실함은 방패와 손 방패가 되나니

5 너는 밤에 놀램과 낮에 흐르는 살과

6 흑암 중에 행하는 염병과 백주에 황폐케 하는 파멸을
두려워 아니하리로다

7 "천인이 네 곁에서, 만인이 네 우편에서 엎드러지나 이 재앙이
네게 가까이 못하리로다"

8 오직 너는 목도하리니 악인의 보응이 네게 보이리로다

9 네가 말하기를 여호와는 나의 피난처시라 하고 지존쟈로
거처를 삼았으므로

10 화가 네게 미치지 못하며 재앙이 네 장막에 가까이 오지 못하리니

11 저가 너를 위하여 그 사자들을 명하사 네 모든 길에 너를
지키게 하심이라

12 저희가 그 손으로 너를 붙들어 발이 돌에 부딪히지 않게 하리로다

13 네가 사자와 독사를 밟으며 젊은 사자와 뱀을 발로 누르리로다

14 하나님이 가라사대 저가 나를 사랑한즉 내가 저를 건지리라
저가 내 이름을 안즉 내가 저를 높이리라

15 저가 내게 간구하리니 내가 응답하리라 저희 환난 때에 내가
저와 함께하여 저를 건지고 영화롭게 하리라

16 내가 잠수함으로 저를 만족케 하며 나의 구원으로
보이리라 하시도다

Modern Greek Holy Bible

Psalms / Ψαλμοί οι

1 ΑΥΤΟΣ που κατοικεί κάτω από τη σκέπη τού Υψίστου, κάτω από τη σκιά του Παντοκράτορα θα διαμένει.

2 Θα λέω στον Κύριο: Εσύ είσαι καταφυγή μου, και φρούριό μου· Θεός μου· σ' αυτόν θα ελπίζω.

3 Επειδή, αυτός θα σε λυτρώνει από την παγίδα των κυνηγών, και από θανατηφόρο λοιμό.

4 Με τα φτερά του θα σε σκεπάζει, και κάτω από τις φτερούγες του θα είσαι ασφαλής η αλήθεια του είναι πανοπλία και ασπίδα.

5 Από φόβο νυχτερινό δεν θα φοβάσαι, την ημέρα από βέλος που πετάει άσκοπα·

6 από θανατικό, που περπατάει στο σκοτάδι από όλεθρο, που ερημώνει ιες το μεσημέρι.

7 Χιλιάδα θα πέφτει από τα αριστερά σου, και μυριάδα από τα δεξιά σου· όμως, σε σένα δεν θα πλησιάζουν.

8 Μονάχα με τα μάτια σου θα θωρείς, και θα βλέπεις την ανταπόδοση των ασεβών.

9 Επειδή, εσύ, τον Κύριο, την ελπίδα μου, τον Ύψιστο, έκανες καταφύγιό σου,

10 κακό δεν θα συμβαίνει σε σένα, και μάστιγα δεν θα πλησιάζει στη σκηνή σου.

11 Επειδή, τους αγγέλους του θα προστάξει για σένα, για να σε διαφυλάττουν σε όλους τούς δρόμους σου.

12 Θα σε σηκώνουν επάνω στα χέρια τους, για να μη προσκόψεις το πόδι σου σε πέτρα.

13 Θα πατήσεις επάνω σε λιοντάρι και επάνω σε οχιά θα καταπατήσεις λιονταράκι και δράκοντα.

14 Επειδή, έβαλε την αγάπη του σε μένα, γι' αυτό θα τον λυτρώσω θα τον υψώσω, επειδή γνώρισε το όνομά μου.

15 Θα με επικαλείται και θα τον εισακούω· μαζί του θα είμαι στη θλίψη θα τον λυτρώνω, και θα τον δοξάζω.

16 Θα τον χορτάσω από μακρότητα ημερών, και θα δείξω σ' αυτόν τη σωτηρία μου.

Finnish Holy Bible

Psalmit 91

1 Joka Korkeimman suojassa istuu ja Kaikkivaltiaan varjossa yöpyy,

2 se sanoo: "Herra on minun turvani ja linnani, hän on minun Jumalani, johon minä turvaan".

3 Sillä hän päästää sinut linnustajan paulasta, turmiollisesta rutosta.

4 Sulillansa hän sinua suojaa, ja sinä saat turvan hänen siipiensä alla; hänen uskollisuutensa on kilpi ja suojus.

5 Et sinä pelkää yön kauhuja, et päivällä lentävää nuolta,

6 et ruttoa, joka pimeässä kulkee, et kulkutautia, joka päiväsydännä häviötä tekee.

7 Vaikka tuhat kaatuisi sinun sivultasi, kymmenen tuhatta oikealta puoleltasi, ei se sinuun satu.

8 Sinun silmäsi saavat vain katsella ja nähdä, kuinka jumalattomille kostetaan.

9 Sillä: "Sinä, Herra, olet minun turvani". Korkeimman olet sinä ottanut suojaksesi.

10 Ei kohtaa sinua onnettomuus, eikä vitsaus lähesty sinun majaasi.

11 Sillä hän antaa enkeleilleen sinusta käskyn varjella sinua kaikilla teilläsi.

12 He kantavat sinua käsillänsä, ettet jalkaasi kiveen loukkaisi.

13 Sinä kuljet leijonan ja kyykäärmeen ylitse, sinä tallaat nuorta jalopeuraa ja lohikäärmettä.

14 "Koska hän riippuu minussa kiinni, niin minä hänet pelastan; minä suojelen hänet, koska hän tuntee minun nimeni.

15 Hän huutaa minua avuksensa, ja minä vastaan hänelle, minä olen hänen tykönänsä, kun hänellä onahdistus, minä vapahdan hänet ja saatan hänet kunniaan.

16 Minä ravitsen hänet pitkällä iällä ja suon hänen nähdä antamani pelastuksen."

Bíbila Envagèlica Catalana

Salms 91

1 Qui habita a l'empara de l'Al-tíssim, i reposa a l'ombra de l'Omnipotent,

2 diu al Senyor: Refugi i castell meu, el meu Déu, en qui confio!

3 Ell et lliurarà del llaç del caçador i de tribulació desgraciada;

4 t'abriga amb les seves plomes i et cobreixes sota les seves ales: la seva fidelitat t'és per escut i de-fensa.

5 No has de témer la basarda de la nit, ni la sageta que vola de dia,

6 ni la pesta que s'infiltra a les fos-ques o la plaga que devasta a migdia.

7 Ni que caiguin vora teu un miler, o deu mil al teu costat, a tu res no et tocarà.

8 Només obrint els ulls veuràs la paga dels dolents.

9 Quan dius: "Tu ets, Senyor, el meu refugi", fas de l'Altíssim el teu acull.

10 No et vindrà cap mal, ni cap desgràcia s'atansarà a la teva tenda,

11 perquè ha manat als seus àngels que et guardin en tots els teus ca-mins;

12 et portaran damunt els palmells perquè el teu peu no ensopegui en les pedres;

13 caminaràs damunt l'àspid i l'es-curçó, trepitjaràs el lleó i el drac.

14 "Ja que posa en mi el seu afecte, jo el salvaré, el protegiré perquè reconeix el meu nom.

15 Sempre que m'invoqui jo l'escol-taré; seré amb ell en la tribulació, el salvaré i l'honoraré;

16 el satisfaré de dies perdurables, i fruirà de la meva salvació."

Bulgarian Holy Bible

Psalms/Псалми 91

1 (По слав. 90). Който живее под покрива на Всевишния, Той ще пребъдва под сянката на Всемогъщия.

2 Ще казвам за Господа: Той е прибежище мое и крепост моя, Бог мой, на Когото уповавам.

3 Защото Той ще те избавя от примката на ловеца И от гибелен мор.

4 С перата Си ще те покрива; И под крилата Му ще прибегнеш; Неговата вярност е щит и закрила.

5 Няма да се боиш от нощен страх, От стрелата, която лети денем,

6 От мор, който ходи в тъмнина, От погибел, която опустошава всред пладне.

7 Хиляда души ще падат от страната ти, И десет хиляди до десницата ти, Но до тебе няма да се приближи.

8 Само с очите си ще гледаш, И ще видиш възмездието на нечестивите

9 Понеже ти си казал: Господ е прибежище мое, И си направил Всевишния обиталището си,

10 Затова няма да те сполети никакво зло, Нито ще се приближи язва до шатъра ти.

11 Защото ще заповяда на ангелите Си за тебе Да те пазят във всичките ти пътища.

12 На ръце ще те дигат, Да не би да удариш о камък ногата си.

13 Ще настъпиш лъв и аспид; Ще стъпчеш млад лъв и змия.

14 Понеже той е положил в Мене любовта си, казва Господ, Затова ще го избавя; Ще го поставя в Безопасност (Еврейски: На всичко.), защото е познал името Ми.

15 Той ще Ме призове, и Аз ще го послушам; С него ще съм, когато е в бедствие; ще го избавя и ще го прославя.

16 Ще го наситя с дългоденствие, И ще му покажа спасението, което върша,

Azərbaycan Bibliyası 2008

ZƏBUR 91

1 Haqq-Taalanın pənahında yaşayan, Külli-İxtiyarın kölgəsində oturan insan

2 Rəbb haqqında belə söyləyir: «O mənim sığınacağımdır, qalamdır, Allahımdır, Ona güvənirəm».

3 Bil ki, O səni ovçunun tələsindən, Ağır xəstəliyə düşüb ölməkdən qurtarar.

4 Səni qanadlarının altına alar, Pərlərinin altında sığınacaqsan. Sədaqəti qalxanın, sipərin olar.

5 Nə gecənin kabusundan, Nə də gündüz atılan oxdan,

6 Nə zülmətdə dolanan ağır xəstəlikdən, Nə də günorta məhvedici qırğından qorxmazsan.

7 Yanında min nəfər, Sağında on min nəfər qırılsa, Sənə xətər dəyməz.

8 Gözlərinlə baxacaqsan, Pislərin cəzasını görəcəksən.

9 «Ya Rabb, sığınacağımsan!» dediyin üçün, Haqq-Taalaya sığındığın üçün

10 Şərə düçar olmazsan, Bəla çadırından uzaq qaçar.

11 Allah sənə görə mələklərinə əmr edər ki, Gedəcəyin hər yerdə səni qorusunlar,

12 Səni əlləri üstündə aparsınlar, Ayağın bir daşa dəyməsin.

13 Şiri, gürzəni ayaqlayarsan, Gənc aslanı, əfi ilanı tapdalayarsan.

14 «Mən Rəbbi sevdiyinə görə onu azad edəcəyəm, İsmimi tanıdığına görə onu yüksəldəcəyəm.

15 Məni çağırarkən ona cavab verəcəyəm, Dar günündə ona yar olacağam, Onu xilas edib şərəfə-şana çatdıracağam.

16 Onu uzun ömürlə doyduracağam, Ona qurtuluşumu göstərəcəyəm>>.

Elizen Arteko Biblia

Salmoak 91

1 Goi-goikoaren aterpean bizi zaren horrek, gaua Ahaltsuaren itzalpean ematen duzun horrek,

2 esazu: «Oi Jauna, zu ene babesleku eta gaztelu; ene Jainko, zuregan dut uste on!>>

3 Berak libratuko zaitu ehiztariaren saretik eta izurri galgarritik.

4 Bere hegalpean emango dizu gerizpe, haren lumapea izango duzu babesleku, haren besoa babeski eta koraza.

5 Ez diozu beldurrik izango gauaren izuari, ez egunez jaurtitako geziari;

6 ez ilunpetan zabaltzen den izurriari, ez egun-argitan jotzen duen gaitzari.

7 Zure ezkerraldean mila, zure eskuinaldean hamar mila erorita ere, zu ez zaitu joko.

8 Begiak zabaldu orduko ikusiko duzu gaiztoen zigor-ordaina,

9 Jauna hartu baituzu babesleku, Goi-goikoa bizileku.

10 Ez zaizu zoritxarrik gertatuko, ez da zure etxera hondamenik iritsiko.

11 Bere aingeruei aginduko die zu nonahi ere zaintzeko.

12 Besoetan eramango zaituzte, harriekin estropezu egin ez dezazun.

13 Suge pozoitsuen gainean ibiliko zara, basapiztiak oinazpian hartuko.

14 <<Niri atxikia dagoenez gero, onik aterako dut, toki seguruan jarriko, aitortzen nauelako.

15 Dei egitean, erantzun egingo diot. Berekin izango nau larrialdian: libratu egingo dut eta ohorez jantziko.

16 Bizitza luze eta betea emango diot eta neure salbamena gozaraziko».

Salmo 91 Cebuano Bible

Ang Pulong Sa Dios

Ang Dios Atong Tigpanalipod

1 Si bisan kinsa nga mangayo sa pagpanalipod sa Labing Halangdong Dios nga Makagagahom, panalipdan niya.

2 Makaingon siya[a] sa Ginoo, "Ikaw ang akong tigpanalipod ug lig-ong tagoanan.

Ikaw ang akong Dios nga ginasaligan."

3 Luwason ka gayod niya gikan sa mga lit-ag ug sa makapatay nga mga balatian.

4 Panalipdan ka niya sama sa usa ka langgam nga nagapanalipod sa iyang mga piso ilalom sa iyang mga pako.

Sa iyang pagkamatinumanon, panalipdan ka niya ug labanan.

5-6 Dili ka angayng mahadlok sa mga makalilisang nga mga panghitabo, sa mga motakboy nga mga balatian, ug sa mga katalagman nga moabot—sa gabii man o sa adlaw.

7 Bisan linibo pa ka mga tawo ang mangamatay sa imong palibot, ikaw dili maunsa.

8 Makita mo na lang kon unsaon pagsilot ang daotang mga tawo.

9 Tungod kay gihimo mo mang dalangpanan ang Ginoo, ang Labing Halangdong Dios nga akong tigpanalipod,

10 walay kalamidad o katalagman nga moabot kanimo o sa imong panimalay.

11 Kay sugoon sa Dios ang iyang mga anghel sa pagbantay kanimo bisan asa ka moadto.

12 Sakwaton ka nila aron dili masamad ang imong tiil sa mga bato.[b]

13 Tumban mo ang mga liyon ug ang malala nga mga bitin.

14 Miingon ang Dios, "Luwason ko ug panalipdan ang nagahigugma ug nagaila kanako.

15 Kon motawag siya kanako, tubagon ko siya;

kon anaa siya sa kalisod, ubanan ko siya;

luwason ko siya ug pasidunggan.

16 Hatagan ko siyag taas nga kinabuhi,

ug ipakita ko kaniya kon unsaon ko siya pagluwas."

Footnotes

91:2 siya: Mao kini sa Septuagint ug sa Syriac; apan sa Hebreo, ako.

91:12 Sakwaton… bato: Ang buot ipasabot, Panalipdan ka nila aron dili ka maunsa.

Fijian Holy Bible

Psalms/Same 91

1 O koya sa tiko ena yasana vuni nei Koya sa Cecere sara, ena vakarurugi tikoga ena yalovalo i Koya sa Kaukauwa.

2 Au sa tukuna ena vuku i Jiova, "Na noqui Drodro kei na noqu Bai ni valu; na noqu Kalou, sai Koya ga au sa vakadinata."

3 Sa dina, ena vakabulai iko mal na nodra vere kece na dauvelveretaki kei na veitauvi ni mate ca kecega.

4 Ena vakarurugi iko ena Tabana, ena nomu i drodro na ruku ni Tabana; na Nona Dina, ena nomu i Sasabai.

5 O na sega ni rerevaka na ka dauvelvakarerei ena bogi, se na gasau sa vuka voli ena siga,

6 Se na mate ca sa lako voli ena butobuto, Se na veivakarusai sa toka vuni ena sigalevu.

7 Eudolu era na bale e yasamu, ka tini na udolu ena ligamu i matau. Ena sega e dua me na torovi iko mal.

8 Ena matamu dina ga, o na raica nai sau ni nodra i valavala na tamata ca.

9 Baleta ni o sa vakatara me nomu i Drodro o Jiova kel Koya sa cecere sara me nomuni tikotiko,

10 Ena sega i tarai iko na ca se dua na mate ca me torova mai na nomu i tikotiko;

11 Ni na soli ira na Nona agilosi me ra lewa ena vukumu, ka maroroi iko ena gauna kecega.

12 Era na keveti iko cake ena ligadra, De qai mavoa na yavamu ena vatu.

13 O na butuki ira na laioni kei gata, o ira na luve ni laioni kei na gata, o na butu qaqia.

14 "Baleta ni sa vagolea mai vei Au na nona loloma, o koya oqo, Au na vakabulai koya ka vakacerecerel koya, ni sa Kila na Yacaqu.

15 Ena qai kaci mai, Au, na qai rogo yani vei koya; Au na laki tiko vata kel koya ena gauna ni lega, Me'u vakabulai koya ka dokai koya.

16 Au na sotavi koya ena bula balavu, ka vakaraitaka vua na Noqu veivakabulai."

Kitab Sutji

Jabur 91

1 Wong kang dumunung ana ing pangaubane Kang Mahaluhurlan nginep ing pangayomane Kang Mahakuwasa,

2 iku bakal nyebut marang Yehuwah mangkene: "Pangungsen saha beteng kawula, Gusti Allah kawula ingkang kawula andelaken."

3 Sanyata Panjenengane iku kang bakal nguwalake kowe saka ing jirete juru pikat, lan saka pageblug kang mbilaeni.

4 kowe bakal dikemuli kalawan elare,bakal diayomi ing sangisoring siwiwine,kasetyane iku minangka tameng lan pager tembok.

5 Kowe ora usah wedi marang pagiris ing wayah bengi, marang panah kang lumepes ing wayah awan,

6 marang pageblug kang lumaku ana ing pepeteng,tuwin marang lelara pes kang ngamuk ing wayah sore.

7 Sanadyan ing sandhingmu ana wong kang ambruk sewu, sarta sepuluh ewu ana ing tengenmu,ewadene kowe dhewe ora bakal ketaman;

8 iku mung koksawang kalawan mripatmu dhewe bae, lan ndeleng piwales marang para wong duraka.

9 Amarga Pangeran Yehuwah iku dadi pangayomanmu,Kang Mahaluhur iku wus kokdadekake pangaubanmu,

10 Kowe ora bakal katempuh ing bilai,sarta ora ana wewelak kang nyedhaki tarubmu;

11 awit Pangeran bakal ndhawuhi para malaekate ing ngatase kowe,supaya rumeksa marang kowe ana ing sakehing dalanmu.

12 Kowe bakal ditadhahi ing tangane,supaya kowe aja nganti kesandhung ing watu.

13 Singa lan ula bedhudhak bakal padha koklangkahi,singa nom lan ula naga bakal kokidak-idak.

14 "Sanyata, sarehne rumaket marang Ingsun, mulane bakal Sunluwari,bakal Sunpageri santosa awit wanuh marang asmaningSun.

15 Yen sesambat marang Ingsun bakal Sunsembadani,ing sajroning karubedan bakal Sunkanthi,bakal Sunentasake lan Sunluhurake,

16 bakal Sunwaregi kalawan umur dawa,lan karahayoningSun bakal Suntedahake marang dheweke."

Khmer Holy Bible

Psalms / ទំនុកដំកើង 91

1 អ្នកណាដែលនៅជាប់ក្នុងទីកំបាំង នៃព្រះដ៏ខ្ពស់បំផុត នោះនឹងបានឈរនៅក្រោមម្លប់នៃព្រះដ៏មានឫទ្ធិ ព្រះចេស្ដា។

2 ឯទូលបង្គំនឹងពោលពីព្រះរបស់វិមា ទ្រង់ជាទីពឹងពំនាក់ ជាបន្ទាយនៃទូលបង្គំ គឺជាព្រះនៃទូលបង្គំហើយ ទូលបង្គំទុកចិត្តនឹងទ្រង់។

3 ៣ ពិតជាកេាជាទ្រង់នឹងដួយរួចឯង ពីលប់របស់នាយព្រាន ហើយពីសេចក្ដីអាចែលទាំឡ្បអន្ទរាយ

4 ទ្រង់នឹងគ្របលងដោយស្លាបទ្រង់ ហើយឯនឹងជ្រកនៅក្រោមចំណងស្លាបរបស់ទ្រង់ សេចក្ដីពិតរបស់ទ្រង់ជាខែល ហើយជាអាវក្រោះ

5 ឯនឹងមិនខ្លាចឡើយឡើយ នោះទាំសេចក្ដីនៃ្ងខ្លាចនៅពេលយប់ ឬព្រួញដែលហើរនៅពេលថ្ងៃ

6 ឬសេចក្ដីរោគាដែលតែចមនៅក្នុងទីងងឹត ឬសេចក្ដីវិនាសដែលបំផ្លាញនៅពេលថ្ងៃត្រង់ផង

7 នឹងមានមនុស្សរាប់ពាន់នៃលួចស្លាប់នៅក្បែរឯង ហើយមួយម៉ឺននាក់ទៅមានខែស្ដាំខ្លួនៃរ តែសេចក្ដីនោះនឹងមិនមកដល់ឯងឡើយ

8 ឯនឹងបានក្រឡេកឃើញការតបស្នង ឯលពួកមនុស្សអាប្រាក់ ដោយផ្ទាល់ភ្នែករបស់ឯណេរទេ

9 ពីព្រោះឯបានថា ព្រះយេហូវ៉ាជាទីពឹងជ្រកនៃឯង គឺបានឯកព្រះដ៏ខ្ពស់បំផុតជាទីលំនៅរបស់ឯង

10 ដ៍ានេនោះ នឹងគ្មានសេចក្ដីអាក្រក់ណាកើតដល់ឯ ឯលឯងឡើយ ក៏គ្មានរោគាណាមកជិតទីលំនៅរបស់ឯងដែរ

11 ដ្បិតទ្រង់នឹងបង្គាប់ដល់ពួកទេវតារបស់ទ្រង់ ពីដំណើរឯង ឲ្យបានថែរក្សាឯ ក្នុងគ្រប់ទាំងផ្លូវរបស់ឯង

12 ទេវតាទាំងនោះនឹងទ្រងឯងដោយដៃ ក្រែងជើងឯងទង្គិចនឹងថ្

13 ឯនឹងជាន់លើទាំងសត្វសឹង្ហ និងពសហាងមានពស ឯលិង្សត្វ នឹងនាគ នោះឯនឹងអាចជាន់ស្ទើរដោយជើងបាន។

14 ៣ ដោយព្រោះរាបានយកអញ្ញាទីស្រឡាញ់ នោះអញ្ញានឹងដួយឲ្យរួច អញ្ញានឹងត់ងឡើងឈ្មោះឯខ្ពស់ ពីព្រោះជាបានស្គាល់ឈ្មោះអញ្ញ

15 កនឹងអំការមាដល់អញ្ញ ហើយអញ្ញនឹងឆ្លើយតប អញ្ញនឹងនៅជាមួយនឹងក្នុងគ្រាកុវ័លបាក់ កំនឹងដើរឲ្យរួចចេញ ប៉ិយនឹងលើកមុខឲ្យ

16 អញ្ញនឹងឲ្យរស់្បូចិត្តនោយអាយុយឺនៃឯ ហើយនឹងបង្ហាញ្ញឲ្យឃើញសេចក្ដីសង្រ្គោះរបស់អញ្ញ។

A. Rubšio ir Č. Kavaliausko vertimas be Antrojo Kanono knygų (LBD- KAN)

Psalmynas 91

1 Kas tik gyvena Aukščiausiojo pastogėje, pasilieka Visagalio pavėsy.

2 Jis sakys VIEŠPAČIUI: „Mano Dieve, mano prieglauda ir tvirtove, pasitikiu tavimi!"

3 Juk tai jis išgelbės tave nuo medžiotojo kilpos ir nuo mirtį nešančio maro.

4 Savo sparnų plunksnomis jis uždengs tave, - po jo sparnais rasi prieglaudą. Jo ištikimybė – dengiantis skydas.

5 Nereikės tau bijoti nakties siaubo nei strėlės, iššautos dieną,

6 nei maro, sėlinančio tamsoje, nei rykštės, niokojančios vidudienį.

7 Nors tūkstantis kristų tavo kairėje ir dešimt tūkstančių - dešinėje, tavęs niekas nepasieks.

8 Tu žiūrėsi ir matysi, kaip baudžiami nedorėliai.

9 Tu pasirinkai VIEŠPATĮ savo prieglauda, Aukščiausiąjį savo užuovėja,

10 todėl neištiks tavęs žala, nepalies tavo palapinės nelaimė,

11 nes jis palieps savo angelams saugoti tave visur, kad ir kur tu eitum.

12 Savo rankomis jie neš tave, kad kojos į akmenį neužsigautum.

13 Tu sumindžiosi liūtą ir gyvatę, sutrypsi liūtuką ir slibiną.

14 „Kas mane myli, tą gelbėsiu; saugosiu jį, nes jis žino mano vardą.

15 Kai jis šauksis manęs, išklausysiu, būsiu su juo varge, išgelbėsiu ir pagerbsiu.

16 Pasotinsiu jį ilgu amžiumi, pagirdysiu savo išganymu".

Luganda Holy Bible

Zabbuli 91

1 Atuula mu kifo eky'ekyama eky'oyo ali waggluu ennyo Ye anaabeeranga wansi w'ekisiikirize eky'Omuyinza w'ebintu byonna.

2 Naayogeranga ku Mukama nti Oyo kye kiddukiro kyange, era kye kigo kyange: Katonda wange gwe nneesiga.

3 Kubanga oyo ye anaakulokolanga mu mutego ogw'omuyizzi, Ne mu kawumpuli omubi.

4 Anaakubikkangako n'ebiwaawaatiro bye, Era wansi w'ebyoya bye w'onoddukiranga: Amazima ge ye ngabo, ge gakuuma.

5 Tootyenga Iwa ntiisa ya kiro Newakubadde akasaale akagenda emisana;

6 Olw'olumbe olutambulira mu kizikiza, Newakubadde olw'okuzikiriza okufaafaaganya mu ttuntu.

7 Abantu olukumi baligwira ku lubiriizi Iwo, Era akakumi ku mukono gwo ogwa ddyo; Tekulikusemberera ggwe.

8 Naye olitunula n'amaaso go, Oliraba empeera y'ababi.

9 Kubanga ggwe, ai Mukama, oli kiddukiro kyange Omufudde oyo ali waggulu ennyo ekigo kyo w'otuula;

10 Tewali kabi akalikubaako, so tewali kibonoobono ekirisemberera eweema yo.

11 Kubanga alikulagiririza bamalayika be, Bakukuume mu makubo go gonna.

12 Balikuwanirira mu mikono gyabwe, Oleme okwesittala ekigere kyo ku jjinja.

13 Olirinnya ku mpologoma ne ku ssalambwa; Olisamba empologoma ento n'omusota wansi w'ebigere byo.

14 Kubanga antaddeko okwagala kwe, kyendiva mmuwonya: Ndimugulumiza waggulu, kubanga amanyi erinnya lyange.

15 Alinkaabira, nange ndimuyita; Naabeeranga wamu naye bw'anaanakuwalanga: Ndimuwonya, ndimuwa ekitiibwa.

16 Ndimuwangaaza nnyo, ndimukkusa obulamu, Era ndimulaga obulokozi bwange.

1 మహోన్నతుని చాటున నివసించువాడే సర్వశక్తుని నీడను విశ్రమించువాడు.

2 ఆయనే నాకు ఆశ్రయము నా కోట నేను నమ్ము కొను నా దేవుడని నేను యెహోవానుగూర్చి చెప్పుచున్నాను.

3 వేటకాని ఉరిలోనుండి ఆయన నిన్ను విడిపించును నాశనకరమైన తెగులు రాకుండ నిన్ను రక్షించును

4 ఆయన తన రెక్కలతో నిన్ను కప్పును ఆయన రెక్కల క్రింద సేరు ఆశ్రయము కలుగును ఆయన సత్యము, కేడెమును డాలువలె యున్నది.

5 రాత్రివేళ కలుగు భయమునకైనను పగటివేళ ఎగురు బాణమునకైనను

6 చీకటిలో సంచరించు తెగులునకైనను మధ్యాహ్నమందు పాడుచేయు రోగమునకైనను నీవు భయపడకుందువు.

7 నీ ప్రక్కను వేయి మంది పడినను నీ కుడిప్రక్కను పదివేల మంది కూలినను అపాయము నీ యొద్దకురాదు.

8 నీవు కన్నులార చూచుచుండగా భక్తిహీనులకు ప్రతిఫలము కలుగును

9 యెహోవా, నీవే నా ఆశ్రయము అని నీవు మహోన్నతుడైన దేవుని నీకు నివాసస్థలముగా చేసికొనియున్నావు

10 నీకు అపాయమేమియు రాదు ఏ తెగులును నీ గుడారమును సమీపించదు

11 నీ మార్గములన్నిటిలో నిన్ను కాపాడుటకు ఆయన నిన్ను గూర్చి తన దూతలను ఆజ్ఞాపించును

12 నీ పాదములకు రాయి తగులకుండ వారు నిన్ను తమ చేతులమీద ఎత్తి పట్టుకొందురు

13 నీవు సింహములను నాగుపాములను త్రొక్కెదవు కొదమ సింహములను భుజంగములను అణగ ద్రొక్కె దవు.

14 అతడు నన్ను ప్రేమించుచున్నాడు గనుక నేనతని తప్పించెదను అతడు నా నామము నెరిగినవాడు గనుక నేనతని ఘనపరచెదను

15 అతడు నాకు మొఱ్ఱపెట్టగా నేనతనికి ఉత్తరమిచ్చె దను శ్రమలో నేనతనికి తోడై యుండెదను అతని విడిపించి అతని గొప్ప చేసెదను

16 దీర్ఘాయువు చేత అతనిని తృప్తిపరచెదను నా రక్షణ అతనికి చూపించెదను.

Turkmen Holy Bible

Zebur 91

1 Beýik Hudaýyň penasynda ýaşaýan ynsan Gudratygüýçliniň kölegesini mesgen ediner.

2 Rebbe diýerin: «Meniň penam hem-de berkitmäm, meniň Hudaýym, özümiň bil baglaýanym».

3 Ol halas eder seni awçyň torundan hem-de heläkleýji mergiden.

4 Ol perleri bilen seni basyrar; ganatlarynyň astynda pena taparsyň, Onuň wepadarlygy galkan, sowutdyr.

5 Gorkmarsyň gijäniň howp-hataryndan ýa-da gündiz uçýan peýkamdan,

6 tümlükde assyrynlyk bilen gelýän mergiden ýa günortan çagy tozdurýan weýrançylykdan.

7 Gapdalynda müň adam, sagyňda on müň adam ýykylar, emma bu zatlar saňa ýanaşmaz.

8 Sen gözleriň bilen ýöne gararsyň, erbetleriň jezalaryny görersiň.

9 Sen Rebbe: «Meniň penamsyň» diýip, Beýik Hudaýy özüňe mesgen edindiň.

10 Şoňa göra ýamanlyk saňa asla yanaşmaz, bela-beter çadyrynyň ýanyna gelmez.

11 Seni ähli ýollaryňda goramak üçin, perişdelerine sen babatda Ol emr eder.

12 Aýagyň daşa büdremez ýaly, olar seni ellerinde göterer.

13 Arslany, ýylany sen depgilärsin, ýolbarsy, alahöwreni sen basgylarsyň.

14 Reb diýýär: «Meni söýýänleri halas ederin, adymy bilýänlere pena bolaryn.

15 Meni çagyranlarynda jogap bererin. Muşakgatlarda olar bilen bolaryn, azat edip, şan-şöhrata beslärin.

16 Olara uzak ömür bagyş ederin olara halas edişimi Men görkezerin>>.

Ukrainian Holy Bible

Psalms / Псалми 91

1 Хто живе під покровом Всевишнього, хто в тіні Всемогутнього мешкає,

2 той скаже до Господа: Охороно моя та твердине моя, Боже мій, я надіюсь на Нього!

3 Бо він тебе вирве з тенет птахолова, з моровиці згубної,

4 Він пером Своїм вкриє тебе, і під крильми Його заховаєшся ти! Щит та лук Його правда.

5 Не будеш боятися страху нічного, ані стріли, що вдень пролітає,

6 ані зарази, що в темряві ходить, ані моровиці, що нищить опівдні,

7 впаде тисяча з боку від тебе, і десять тисяч праворуч від тебе, до тебе ж не дійде!...

8 Тільки своїми очима подивишся, і заплату безбожним попобачиш,

9 60 Господа, охорону мою, Всевишнього ти учинив за своє пристановище!

10 Тебе зло не спіткає, і до намету твого вдар не наблизитьея,

11 60 Своїм Анголам Він накаже про тебе, щоб тебе пильнували на всіх дорогах твоїх,

12 на руках вони будуть носити тебе, щоб не вдарив об камінь своєї ноги!

13 На лева й вужа ти наступиш, левчука й крокодила ти будеш топтати!

14 що бажав він Мене, то його збережу, зроблю його сильним, бо знає ім'я Моє він;

15 як він мене кликатиме, то йому відповім, Я з ним буду в недолі, врятую його та прославлю його,

16 і довгістю днів Я насичу його, і він бачити буде спасіння Моє!

Prayer for Salvation

Glory to God!

John 3:16-18 in the Message Bible reads:

This is how much God loved the world: he gave his Son, his one and only Son. And this is why: so that no one need be destroyed; by believing in him, anyone can have a whole and lasting life. God didn't go to all the trouble of sending his Son merely to point an accusing finger, telling the world how it was. He came to help, to put the world right again. Anyone who trusts in him is acquitted; anyone who refuses to trusts in him has long since been under the death sentence without knowing it. And why? Because of that person's failure to believe in the one-of-kind Son of God when introduced to him. Amen

Say this confession from the Bible verses above from the depth of your heart to make Jesus your Savior and Lord, if you have never made him the Lord and Savior of your life or if you have backslidden or wish to rededicate your life to the Lord Jesus, confess this

I confess Lord, that you love the world so very much, and that includes me _____(name)He gave his Son, His One and only Son so that no one needs be destroyed, that includes me if I _____(name)believe will not perish but have everlasting life.

I_____hereby confess with all my heart, with all my soul, with all my mind, with all my strength, that Jesus is the Son of the living God.

He died on the Cross and washed away my sins to save me and resurrected victoriously. I am sorry for all my sins and foolish ways. In the Name of Jesus, I repent of all my sins, in thoughts, word and deeds. I renounce all my evil ways. I thank you for forgiving me and receiving me as your child forever. From this day forward I purpose to live only for you in the light of the gospel. Fill me with your Holy Spirit with the evidence of speaking in tongues. I thank you Lord with all my heart, soul, mind and strength that I am now born again. I am a brand new creature in Christ Jesus. Amen! Hallelujah!

Thank you Lord for connecting me to a spirit filled Church and believers who will help me to grow in the love and admonish of the Lord! Thank you Lord, by grace through faith, You are now my Lord and Savior, my healer, my deliverer, my provider, my wisdom, my strength, my joy, my defender, and my all in all, in Jesus Mighty Name, Amen! Hallelujah (cf John 3:16-18, Romans 10:9-10, Acts 2:21, Ephesians 2:8-9, Luke 13:22-28, 15:11-32, Mark 15-20, Luke 18:18-29)

{Prayer of Salvation written by Pastor Daisy Obi as given by the Holy Spirit to be inserted in her book}